LEARN TO SAIL
IN A WEEKEND

LEARN TO SAIL
IN A WEEKEND

JOHN DRISCOLL

Photography by Peter Chadwick

ALFRED A. KNOPF
New York
1998

A DORLING KINDERSLEY BOOK

This edition is a Borzoi Book published in 1998 by Alfred A. Knopf, Inc.
by arrangement with Dorling Kindersley

Art Editor Vicki James
Project Editor Mary-Clare Jerram
Series Editor James Harrison
Production Controller Meryl Silbert

First published in Great Britain in 1991
by Dorling Kindersley Limited,
9 Henrietta Street, London WC2E 8PS

Library of Congress Cataloging-in-Publication Data
Driscoll, John.
Learn to sail in a weekend / John Driscoll. 1st ed.
p. cm. -- (Learn in a weekend series)
ISBN 0-375-70321-7
1. Sailing I. Title II. Series
GV811.D68 1991
796.352--dc20 90-53420
CIP

Computer page make-up by
The Cooling Brown Partnership, UK
Reproduced by Colourscan,
Singapore
Printed and bound in Singapore
by KHL Printing Co Pte Ltd,
Singapore

First American Paperback Edition, June 199

CONTENTS

Introduction 6

PREPARING FOR THE WEEKEND 8

THE WEEKEND COURSE 26

Day 1

Day 2

AFTER THE WEEKEND 78

INTRODUCTION

WELCOME TO SAILING. The aim of *Learn to Sail in a Weekend* is to teach a helmsman and crew the basic techniques of sailing in a course lasting 12 hours over a weekend. By the end of that time you should be able to sail safely in light winds, and be on the right track for more advanced skills in the future. You will never stop learning. I have enjoyed sailing for almost 30 years, and feel there is still more for me to learn.

Of course, there is a good deal more to sailing than the techniques covered in *Learn to Sail in a Weekend*. Perhaps that explains its popularity as a leisure activity for men and women of all ages. Whether you want to reach Olympic standards, or yearn to explore inaccessible areas of the coast, sailing is a sport for life.

JOHN DRISCOLL

PREPARING FOR THE WEEKEND

Before you embark on the weekend course, learn a few basics about the sport on dry land

BEFORE SETTING OUT, THE FIRST THING you need is some special clothing so that you stay warm and dry. However, the most important part of your weekend's preparation, essential to your sailing enjoyment, is to understand that personal buoyancy is vital. Every good sailing school and center will provide personal buoyancy aids in different sizes to the correct international standard. If you are starting with an experienced friend, or learning alone, you will need to acquire a buoyancy aid of your own.

Sailing to keep fit

There is no need to do any physical training before the course. Top-level competitions demand fitness and stamina, but everyone can enjoy recreational sailing. In light winds, wheeling the boat down and up the launching and landing site may be your most strenuous activity. In moderate and strong winds,

Buoyancy aids pp.18-19

Parts of a boat pp.12-13

when the pace is faster, sailing provides good, all-round exercise that can help to keep you fit. If you can swim, you will feel more confident afloat, and be less likely to panic. However, you should never find yourself in a situation where you have to swim very far. Even if you capsize, the golden rule is always to stay with the boat until help arrives.

Learning the ropes

Take time on dry land to familiarize yourself with the different parts of your boat and their function before getting into it. Learn how to tie the five basic nautical knots. *Words in **bold** are given further explanation in the glossary on pages 92-93.*

Laser))

Rudder control pp.22-23

Tying knots pp.14-15

SAILBOAT DESIGN

*Each component of a sailboat
has a particular function*

SAILBOATS have changed considerably from the heavy open
boats of 50 years ago to the sleek designs of today. The
materials used to build them combine strength with
minimum weight and low maintenance, giving you
efficient, exciting sailing with less time spent ashore
keeping the boat in top condition. The parts shown here
are common to almost all sailboats used around the world.

MAST •
Usually made of aluminium alloy, but
sometimes of wood, the **mast** is able to
withstand the incredible loads imposed on
the sails in strong winds. It is normally
stepped on a specially made metal casting
to keep it securely in place.

STANDING RIGGING •
This **mast** is supported by 3 wires:
the **forestay**, leading down to the
bow; and the **2 shrouds**, leading
to either side of the boat.
On some smaller boats
it is freestanding in a
deep maststep.

SPREADERS •
The spreaders are bolted to the
mast at mid-height. They
prevent the mast from bending
too much under load.

HULL
The hull is the basic frame of the sailboat.
Most hulls are GRP (glass-reinforced
plastic) but some are made of
polyethylene, which tends to be
more robust. The surface of the
hull is smooth to reduce water
resistance.

BOW •
Nautical term for the
front of the boat.

Spinnaker chute system – racing option •

• DECK SURFACE
On areas where helmsman and crew sit or
stand, the surface of the deck is molded with a
non-slip pattern.

INHERENT BUOYANCY
Most classes have airtight tanks or polyurethane blocks to provide built-in buoyancy in case of a capsize. Others have inflatable, plastic buoyancy bags that are securely strapped in place.

BOOM •
Made of aluminum alloy, or occasionally of wood, the **boom** extends the **mainsail foot** to maintain the correct sail shape. The **sheets** that control the mainsail are also fixed to the boom.

• STERN
Nautical term for the back of the boat.

• MAINSHEET
The principal rope for controlling the sail, the **mainsheet** is usually guided to the center of the boat. In a few classes it works on a pulley system at the **stern**.

RUDDER •
Providing one of the ways of steering, the **rudder** is attached securely with special fittings to the **transom** (back edge) of the boat. The strength of its alloy stock (head) and GRP blade enable it to withstand heavy loads in windy conditions.

• TILLER
The **rudder** is controlled by the **tiller**, which has a long extension so that you can steer the boat while sitting well out. When made of alloy, which is a cold material to handle, the tiller extension is fitted with a comfortable, non-slip rubber grip, like that on a golf club.

• CENTERBOARD
The **centerboard** prevents the boat drifting sideways. It is housed in a case and hinges down below the hull; another type that is called a **daggerboard** slides up and down. As most classes have centerboards, this is the term used throughout the book.

• TOESTRAPS
The helmsman and crew hook their feet under these straps so that they can sit well out to balance the **heeling** effect of the **rig**.

• CABIN
The control center of the boat, the cabin varies in size: racing boats have small ones, while cruisers have larger cabins.

PARTS OF A BOAT

Fittings on a sailboat for the rigging and controls

SMALLER FITTINGS on small boats have evolved for simplicity or, in the case of the racing classes, for maximum efficiency. Those shown here are common to almost all popular classes. Some boats may have extra fittings for controlling **mast** bend and sail shape.

RUDDER FITTINGS •
The **rudder** is bolted to the **stern** with a pair of stainless steel pintles (pins) and gudgeons (rings).

SELF-BAILER •
The self-bailer is opened when the boat is under way, and closed when it is stationary.

MAINSHEET BLOCK •
This final **block** in the **mainsheet** system may have a ratchet action. In strong winds the ratchet is on; in light weather the ratchet is off.

CHAINPLATE •
A stainless steel plate securely bolted to the hull beside the **shrouds**. Adjustable rigging plates allow you to increase the tension of the shrouds

• CUNNINGHAM
This simple system
enables you to adjust the
tension in the leading
edge of the sail, and
thus control the sail
shape for different
wind speeds.

• KICKING STRAP
Secured between the **boom** and the bottom
of the **mast**, the **kicking strap** is a multi-
part rope arrangement used to control the
shape of the **mainsail**. It is easily
adjusted under way.

• JIB FAIRLEAD
The **jib** sheets are
fed through
fairleads to give
the correct
direction of pull.

• HALYARD
Used to hoist the sail, the
halyard is made of wire
with a rope end for easy
handling. It is secured
on to a **halyard** rack
or **cleat** (special
hook) at the base of
the **mast** when the
sail is hoisted.

SHACKLES •
D-shaped stainless steel fittings
with removable screw-pin fastenings,
shackles are used for securing and connecting
sails and wires all over the boat.

TYING NAUTICAL KNOTS

How to tie five basic nautical knots

BEFORE YOU EMBARK ON YOUR weekend sailing, it is essential to know how to tie the five knots shown on these pages, and how to coil rope. Each knot is intended for a particular purpose and, used at the right time in the right place, each one is secure, yet can be undone quickly.

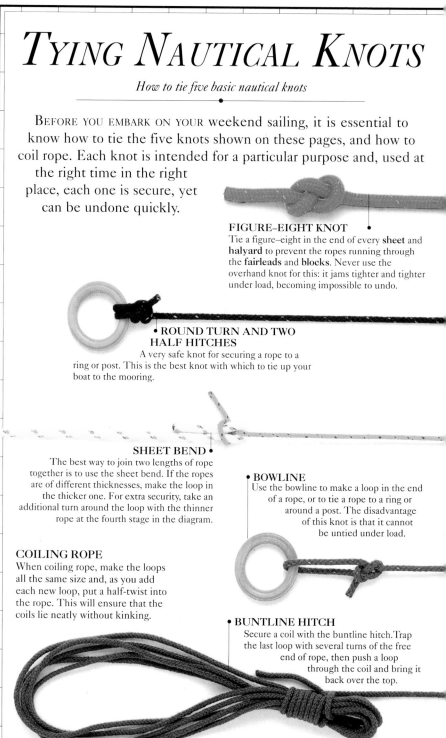

FIGURE–EIGHT KNOT
Tie a figure–eight in the end of every **sheet** and **halyard** to prevent the ropes running through the **fairleads** and **blocks**. Never use the overhand knot for this: it jams tighter and tighter under load, becoming impossible to undo.

ROUND TURN AND TWO HALF HITCHES
A very safe knot for securing a rope to a ring or post. This is the best knot with which to tie up your boat to the mooring.

SHEET BEND
The best way to join two lengths of rope together is to use the sheet bend. If the ropes are of different thicknesses, make the loop in the thicker one. For extra security, take an additional turn around the loop with the thinner rope at the fourth stage in the diagram.

BOWLINE
Use the bowline to make a loop in the end of a rope, or to tie a rope to a ring or around a post. The disadvantage of this knot is that it cannot be untied under load.

COILING ROPE
When coiling rope, make the loops all the same size and, as you add each new loop, put a half-twist into the rope. This will ensure that the coils lie neatly without kinking.

BUNTLINE HITCH
Secure a coil with the buntline hitch. Trap the last loop with several turns of the free end of rope, then push a loop through the coil and bring it back over the top.

HANDY HINTS FOR TYING KNOTS

Practice tying these knots at home with a couple of spare lengths of rope until you can do each one without having to follow the diagrams.

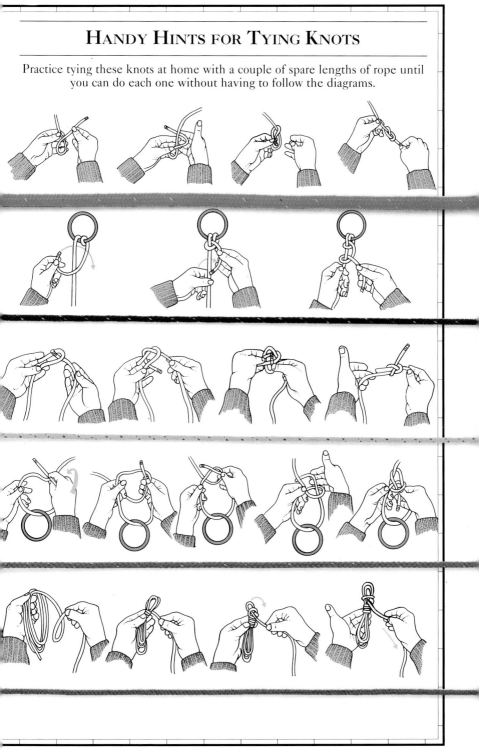

SAILING GEAR

Specialized clothing for warmth and comfort

THERE ARE THREE MAIN TYPES of clothing for small boat sailing: oilskins, wetsuits and drysuits. If you expect to stay more or less dry, lightweight foul weather gear will protect you from wind and spray. If you are sailing a high-performance boat and anticipate getting wet, a wetsuit is ideal. In colder conditions, a drysuit provides total protection from wind and water. The all-year-round sailor will probably have all three, depending on expected weather conditions and type of boat.

• GLOVES
Sailing gloves have non-slip palms and fingers. The full gloves shown here keep your hands warmest, but fingerless mittens allow greater dexterity.

HAT •
On cold days a great deal of body heat is lost through the head. Wear a warm, close-fitting hat to increase comfort.

FOUL-WEATHER GEAR •
Modern, synthetic foul-weather gear provides a wind- and waterproof layer over everyday clothes. A smock avoids a front-fastening zipper – a potential source of leaks – but a zipped jacket is easier to get on and off. Both have waterproof seals at neck and wrists. Chest-high trousers are held up by suspenders. A double layer of material around the knees reduces wear.

DRYSUIT •
A drysuit is made from waterproof material, with tight seals at neck and wrists so that you remain completely dry. This one has integral socks; other types have ankle seals. Wear sailing shoes or boots with both types. A drysuit should not be too tight across the shoulders and chest. When fitting, measure yourself over what you plan to wear underneath – warm clothing in cold weather, polar clothing in extreme conditions. Before going afloat, expel any trapped air: crouch right down while venting the neck seal. If you don't do this, the drysuit will flap around you, and could make swimming difficult if you fall in.

CARE

Rinse your wetsuit well after each sail, even if you haven't been in the water. Check the zipper if you are sailing in salt water.

WETSUIT

Wear a wetsuit over a t-shirt, a bathing suit or trunks, or nothing at all. When you become wet, a thin layer of water is trapped between the synthetic Neoprene material and your skin. This water is quickly warmed up to near body temperature. A wetsuit must fit very closely to be effective, so make sure you are measured properly before buying one.

COMBINED CLOTHES

The best and most popular combination of wetsuit garments is sleeveless long johns (suitable for warmer days) with a long-sleeved bolero jacket for added protection in colder weather. Other designs include summer shorties (no legs or sleeves) and long-sleeved one-piece suits. Some types have detachable sleeves for greater versatility. Summer wetsuits are made of thinner material than winter suits, and are thus more flexible and comfortable.

TOP LAYER

In windy, cold weather, a lightweight, all-in-one suit worn over your wetsuit prevents windchill. This also protects its material from abrasion.

• BOOTS

Boat boots have non-slip soles, and are ribbed on the top for added grip and comfort under the toestraps.

POINTS ON SAFETY

Sailing is a safe sport, as long as you do not take the environment for granted

A RESPONSIBLE APPROACH to sailing involves wearing the right clothing for safety and comfort, and ensuring that your boat and gear are kept in good condition. Adequate personal buoyancy and good, non-slip footwear are essential for every sailor. Always check the weather forecast before sailing (see p.86). Afterwards, pack the boat away, tidy the ropes and fold the sails to enable you to monitor any necessary repairs. Everyone who goes afloat should be familiar with basic mouth-to-mouth resuscitation techniques.

STAYING AFLOAT

Wear a buoyancy aid or life jacket over your clothes whenever you go sailing.

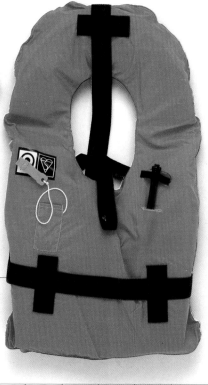

BUOYANCY AID •
This garment provides extra support when you are in the water, and is comfortable and warm to wear. A buoyancy aid allows greater mobility in the boat than a lifejacket. The different sizes relate to the body weight the buoyancy aid can support, so make sure you wear the correct size.

LIFEJACKET •
When fully inflated, a lifejacket will turn an unconscious person on to their back and keep their face clear of the water.

NAUTICAL FOOTWEAR

The right footwear prevents slipping, and damage to the boat: wear deck shoes to launch from a mooring, boots to launch from the shore.

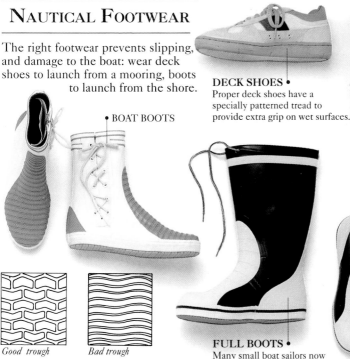

• BOAT BOOTS

DECK SHOES •
Proper deck shoes have a specially patterned tread to provide extra grip on wet surfaces.

Good trough   *Bad trough*

SENSIBLE SOLES
Soft soles with deep, wide troughs allow water to escape from under the tread, so avoid shoes with hard soles and shallow troughs.

FULL BOOTS •
Many small boat sailors now prefer the proper boat boot (above left). This allows in a small amount of water, which heats up to near body temperature so that your feet stay warm. Worn with thermal socks, full boots are ideal for winter sailing.

MOUTH-TO-MOUTH RESUSCITATION

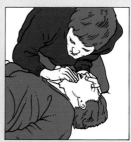

1. Open the victim's airway, clearing any obstructions. Keeping their head well back, jaw forward and mouth well open, pinch the nostrils shut with your fingers and thumb.

2. Take a deep breath, open your mouth wide, and seal your lips around the victim's mouth. Blow firmly but gently into their mouth, while watching to see the chest rise. Repeat.

3. Lift your head away from the victim to watch the chest fall, and to take in more fresh air. Continue ventilation at about 16 times per minute until the victim starts to breathe normally.

HARNESSING THE WIND

Understanding the forces at work on the boat

•

WHEN THE SAIL is angled correctly to the wind, a force acting at
about 90° to the sail – the total sail force – is produced. This drives
the boat forwards, but can also push it sideways, and tip it over. The
extent of this sideways **drag** depends on wind direction. By
adjusting the sails, the **centerboard**, and their own weight, the
helmsman and crew can maximize forward **drive** and minimize
sideways **drag**.

SAIL ANGLE
A 90° total sail force angle
creates **drive** and **drag**.
Sideways drag lessens as
the boat turns further
away from the wind.

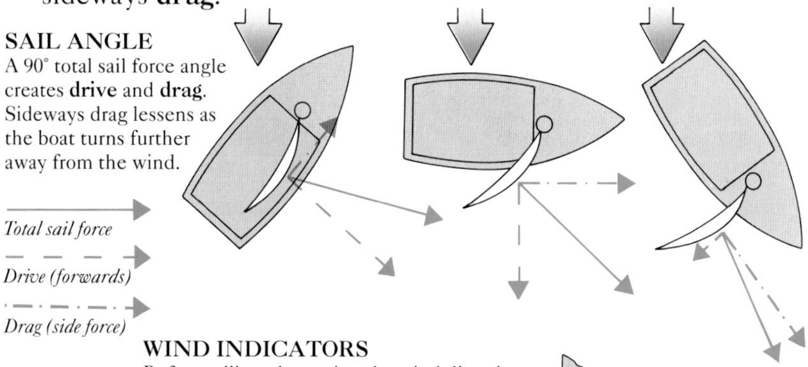

Total sail force

Drive (forwards)

Drag (side force)

WIND INDICATORS
Before sailing, determine the wind direction.
Look at the smoke from chimneys, ripples on
the water, or a burgee (wind indicator) fitted
at the boat's masthead. When sailing, the side
of the boat closest to the wind is called
windward, the side furthest away
leeward.

Burgee

Smoke

Windward

Ripples

Leeward

ACTING FORCES

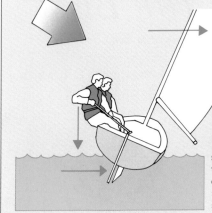

WIND
As the hull and foils – the **rudder** and **centerboard** – resist sideways **drag**, the boat tends to **heel** over.

BODY WEIGHT
The weight of the helmsman and crew is a boat's only ballast, needed for stability.

WATER RESISTANCE
Leeway (the extent of sideways **drag**) varies with wind direction. This drag can be reduced with the **centerboard** and **rudder**.

KEEPING CONTROL

To harness the wind to drive the boat forwards, the helmsman and crew must adjust the sails, the **centerboard**, and their own position each time the boat changes direction.

• CREW AND HELMSMAN
A boat sails most efficiently when it is upright. The helmsman has greatest control and visibility on the **windward** side. The crew keeps the hull flat by sitting to **windward** in strong winds, and to **leeward** in light weather.

• SAILS
A sail works best at only one angle to the wind. Even on a constant course, adjust the sails continually, easing them out until the **luff** (leading edge) begins to flap, and then **sheeting** them in again until the flapping stops.

• CENTERBOARD
The **centerboard** is adjusted according to your course in relation to the wind. When sailing **downwind** it is almost fully raised; when sailing **close-hauled** it is kept down.

STEERING THE BOAT

How to control the direction of the boat

THERE ARE THREE METHODS of controlling the direction in which a boat sails: using the **rudder**; using the sails; and **heeling** the hull. Every rudder movement slows the boat down, so you must understand the other ways of controlling direction.

USING THE RUDDER

The **rudder** gives you the most positive control, but works only when the boat is moving.

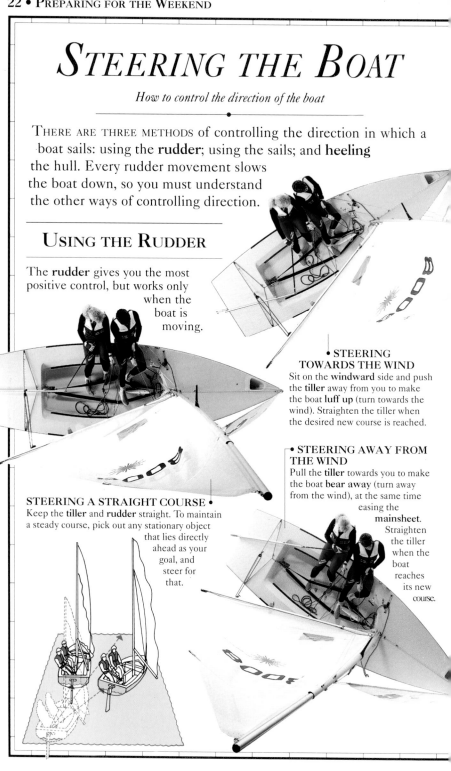

• STEERING TOWARDS THE WIND

Sit on the **windward** side and push the **tiller** away from you to make the boat **luff up** (turn towards the wind). Straighten the tiller when the desired new course is reached.

• STEERING AWAY FROM THE WIND

Pull the **tiller** towards you to make the boat **bear away** (turn away from the wind), at the same time easing the **mainsheet**. Straighten the tiller when the boat reaches its new course.

STEERING A STRAIGHT COURSE •

Keep the **tiller** and **rudder** straight. To maintain a steady course, pick out any stationary object that lies directly ahead as your goal, and steer for that.

USING THE SAILS

When operated independently, the **mainsail** and the **jib** can be used to turn the boat in opposite directions.

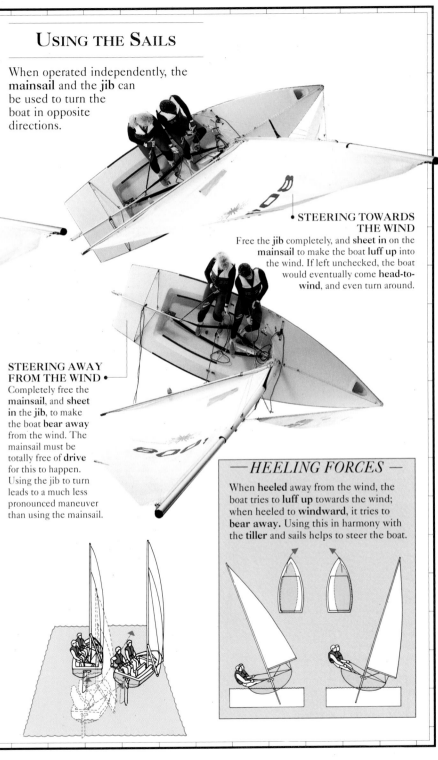

STEERING TOWARDS THE WIND

Free the **jib** completely, and **sheet in** on the **mainsail** to make the boat **luff up** into the wind. If left unchecked, the boat would eventually come **head-to-wind**, and even turn around.

STEERING AWAY FROM THE WIND

Completely free the **mainsail**, and **sheet in the jib**, to make the boat **bear away** from the wind. The mainsail must be totally free of **drive** for this to happen. Using the jib to turn leads to a much less pronounced maneuver than using the mainsail.

—HEELING FORCES—

When **heeled** away from the wind, the boat tries to **luff up** towards the wind; when heeled to **windward**, it tries to **bear away.** Using this in harmony with the **tiller** and sails helps to steer the boat.

POINTS OF SAILING

The different directions in which you can sail

EACH TIME YOU CHANGE COURSE you must adjust the sails and the **centerboard** as the boat's position in relation to the wind alters. Each direction you sail in has a name collectively known as the points of sailing.

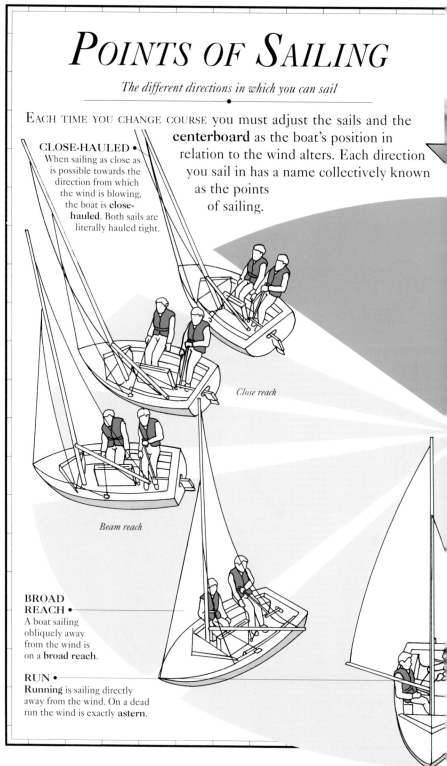

CLOSE-HAULED •
When sailing as close as is possible towards the direction from which the wind is blowing, the boat is **close-hauled**. Both sails are literally hauled tight.

Close reach

Beam reach

BROAD REACH •
A boat sailing obliquely away from the wind is on a **broad reach**.

RUN •
Running is sailing directly away from the wind. On a dead run the wind is exactly **astern**.

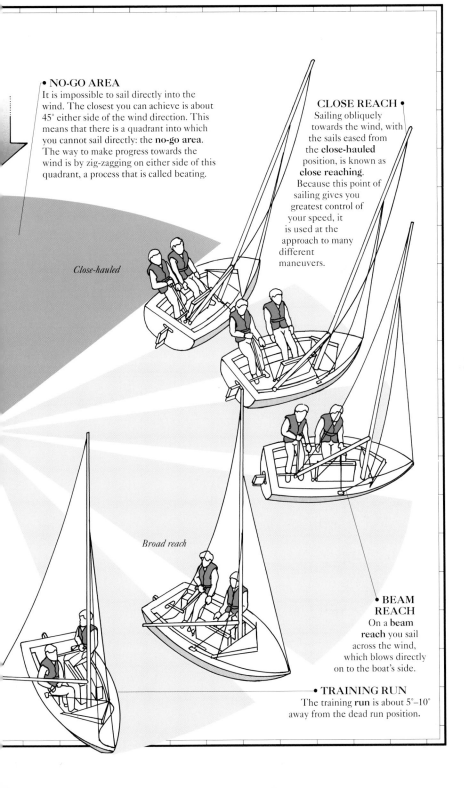

• NO-GO AREA
It is impossible to sail directly into the wind. The closest you can achieve is about 45° either side of the wind direction. This means that there is a quadrant into which you cannot sail directly: the **no-go area**. The way to make progress towards the wind is by zig-zagging on either side of this quadrant, a process that is called beating.

CLOSE REACH •
Sailing obliquely towards the wind, with the sails eased from the **close-hauled** position, is known as **close reaching**. Because this point of sailing gives you greatest control of your speed, it is used at the approach to many different maneuvers.

Close-hauled

Broad reach

• BEAM REACH
On a **beam reach** you sail across the wind, which blows directly on to the boat's side.

• TRAINING RUN
The training **run** is about 5°–10° away from the dead run position.

THE WEEKEND COURSE

An at-a-glance timetable for the 2-day sailing course

THE COURSE IS DIVIDED into 12 skills. Technical terms are highlighted in **bold** and explained in the glossary. Choose a weekend when settled weather and light breezes are forecast. It is safest to start on inland waters, as they have no strong tides or currents. For coastal sailing, pick a time near high or low water, when the tidal stream is slack. Tell someone on land where you are going, and when you plan to return.

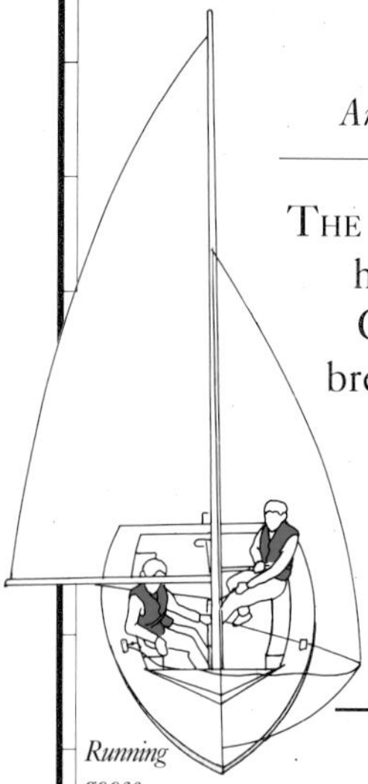

Running goose-winged

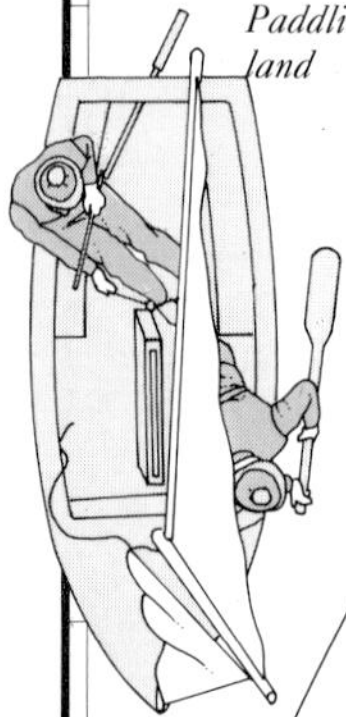

Paddling to land

Broad reach

DAY 1		Hours	Pages
SKILL 1	Rigging	1	28–31
SKILL 2	Launching	¹/₂	32–33
SKILL 3	Leaving land	¹/₂	34–37
SKILL 4	Reaching	1	38–41
SKILL 5	Tacking	1¹/₂	42–47
SKILL 6	Sailing upwind	1	48–51
SKILL 7	Returning to land	¹/₂	52–55

Bearing away

Recovering a capsized boat

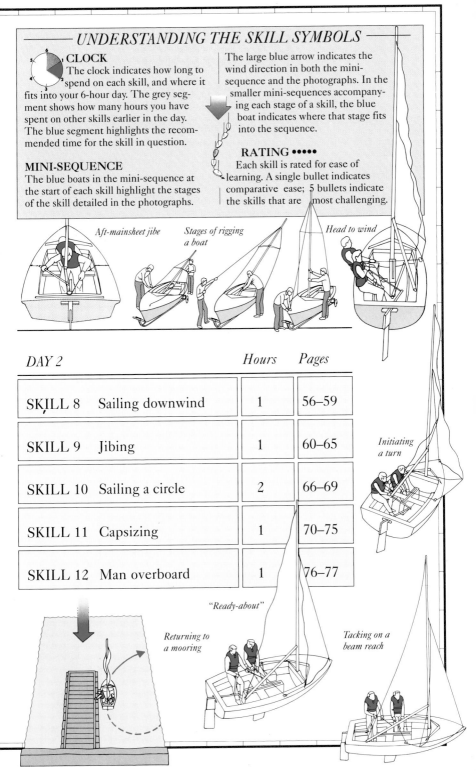

UNDERSTANDING THE SKILL SYMBOLS

CLOCK
The clock indicates how long to spend on each skill, and where it fits into your 6-hour day. The grey segment shows how many hours you have spent on other skills earlier in the day. The blue segment highlights the recommended time for the skill in question.

MINI-SEQUENCE
The blue boats in the mini-sequence at the start of each skill highlight the stages of the skill detailed in the photographs.

The large blue arrow indicates the wind direction in both the mini-sequence and the photographs. In the smaller mini-sequences accompanying each stage of a skill, the blue boat indicates where that stage fits into the sequence.

RATING •••••
Each skill is rated for ease of learning. A single bullet indicates comparative ease; 5 bullets indicate the skills that are most challenging.

Aft-mainsheet jibe

Stages of rigging a boat

Head to wind

DAY 2

		Hours	Pages
SKILL 8	Sailing downwind	1	56–59
SKILL 9	Jibing	1	60–65
SKILL 10	Sailing a circle	2	66–69
SKILL 11	Capsizing	1	70–75
SKILL 12	Man overboard	1	76–77

Initiating a turn

"Ready-about"

Returning to a mooring

Tacking on a beam reach

1 RIGGING

Definition: *Preparing the boat for sailing*

RIG THE BOAT before going afloat. If you have just towed it to the sailing area, this will involve stepping the **mast**. Masts are either stepped on to the deck (see below) or on to the keel (see opposite). Then attach the sails to the **spars**, hoist the sails, and prepare the **rudder** and **tiller**.

OBJECTIVE: Attach all fittings correctly and securely to ensure safety and efficiency afloat. *Rating* ••

Stage 1

STEPPING THE MAST

It is usually easier if one person lifts in the **mast**, while the other stands by to attach the **forestay**. Before stepping the mast, always check that there are no overhead power cables nearby.

MAST •
Lift with your hands comfortably apart, for the best control. Try to keep the **mast** as nearly vertical as possible during the lift, or it will overbalance.

• SHROUDS
With most deck-stepped **masts**, you can attach both **shrouds** to the **chainplates** before lifting the mast into position.

• FORESTAY
Attach the **forestay** after the **mast** is stepped, but do not put any tension on it while the mast is being lifted into place.

HULL •
A slight **bow**-down attitude helps to keep the **mast** in place while you are attaching the **forestay**.

ROPE •
Tidy up all the rope ends so that they do not become trapped under the heel of the **mast** when you step it.

KEEL STEPPING

Many **masts** are held in a gate at deck level, and stepped in the bottom of the boat for extra support.
1. Support the mast while the other person attaches the **shrouds**.
2. Locate the **mast** heel into its fitting and pull on the **forestay** to raise the mast.
3. Attach the forestay to the **bow** fitting. Close the mast gate.

Stage 2

HOISTING THE JIB

If you are **rigging** the boat ashore, the **jib** is usually hoisted before the **mainsail**.

HALYARD RACK •
After hoisting the **jib**, slip the **halyard** on to the toothed **halyard** rack. Coil the rope tail and stow it neatly.

CREW •
Check the **jib halyard** is free. To hoist the sail, pull the halyard's rope tail until the loop in the end of the wire emerges from the **mast** sheave.

• **HALYARD**
Before hoisting the **jib**, shackle the **halyard** to the head of the jib.

JIB FAIRLEADS •
Take the **jib sheets** through their **fairleads** and tie figure–eight knots in the ends.

JIB TACK •
Before hoisting the **jib**, shackle the lower front corner to the **bow** fitting. Keeping the foot of the jib close to the deck improves sailing efficiency.

SKILL

1 MAINSAIL HOISTING
Stage 3

With the **jib** up, prepare to hoist the **mainsail**. Check first you are **head-to-wind**.

HALYARD
Before shackling the **halyard** to the head of the **mainsail** (left), look up the **mast** to check that the halyard is not twisted around the **shrouds**.

• CREW
Feed the **luff** edge into the groove in the back of the **mast**, as the helmsman hoists the **mainsail**.

• MAINSAIL
Once the foot of the sail is attached to the **boom**, flake the sail loosely in the boat to ensure that the **luff** is not twisted, so the sail can be hoisted easily.

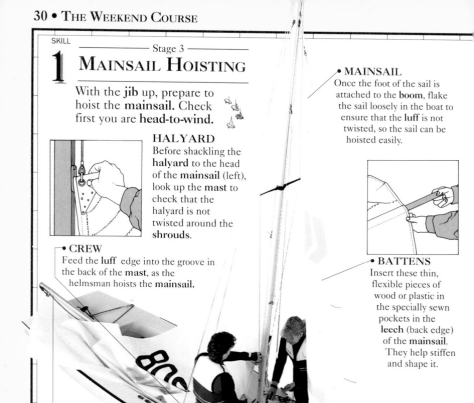

• BATTENS
Insert these thin, flexible pieces of wood or plastic in the specially sewn pockets in the **leech** (back edge) of the **mainsail**. They help stiffen and shape it.

• BOOM
Attach the foot of the sail to the **boom**. Shackle or secure the **tack** (bottom front corner of the sail) to the front of the boom, and tie out the **clew** (back corner) to the boom end.

HELMSMAN •
Pull steadily on the **halyard** to hoist the **mainsail**. **Cleat** or secure the **halyard** on to the rack.

BOOM GROOVE
Although many boats have a loose-footed **mainsail** like the one above, it is more common for the foot of the **mainsail** to be secured along its whole length in a groove in the **boom**.

1. Feed the foot from the **clew** into the **boom**'s forward end.

2. Then secure the **tack** to the **boom** with a pin.

3. Secure the **clew** tightly with a lashing and half hitches.

4. When the sail is up, slot the **boom** to the **mast** at the **gooseneck**.

RIGGING

In two-handed boats, **mainsail** sheeting is arranged either as center-mainsheet or as aft-mainsheet. Each requires different techniques for certain aspects of boat handling.

CENTER-MAINSHEET

Most high-performance boats are center-mainsheet, which allows easier control of the sail. In Lasers, a 2-part sheeting system runs on a traveller across the **stern,** for-ward along the **boom,** down to a ratchet **block**. Other classes have a 3- or 4-part block system between the center of the boom and the **centerboard** case.

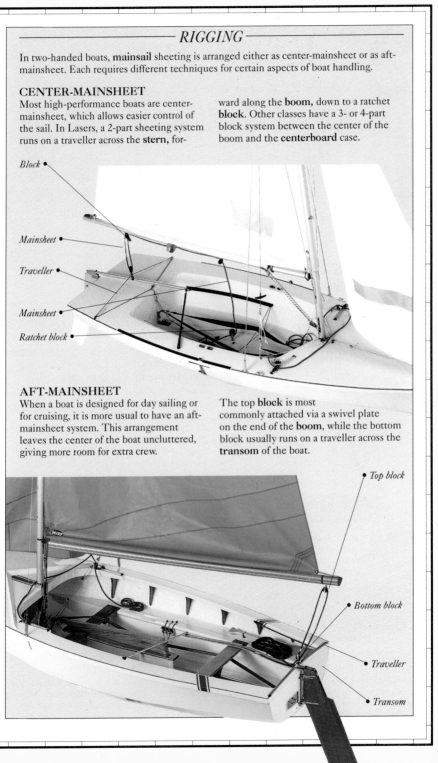

Block

Mainsheet

Traveller

Mainsheet

Ratchet block

AFT-MAINSHEET

When a boat is designed for day sailing or for cruising, it is more usual to have an aft-mainsheet system. This arrangement leaves the center of the boat uncluttered, giving more room for extra crew.

The top **block** is most commonly attached via a swivel plate on the end of the **boom,** while the bottom block usually runs on a traveller across the **transom** of the boat.

Top block

Bottom block

Traveller

Transom

SKILL

2 LAUNCHING

DAY 1

Definition: *Launching the boat without damaging its hull*

MORE DAMAGE IS CAUSED to boat hulls during launching than when they are afloat. If you follow the basic advice given here, however, you will avoid scratches which look bad, slow the boat down, and can lead to more serious hull damage. In this skill the roles of the helmsman and crew are interchangeable.

OBJECTIVE: To launch the boat from its trolley without allowing the hull to come into contact with the ground. *Rating* •

• RUDDER

If the **rudder** has a lifting blade that can be secured when fully raised, attach it before launching the boat. Otherwise, wait until you are afloat.

Stage 1

WHEELING IN

Everything in the boat must be ready before launching. Check that the **transom** and buoyancy tank drain plugs are in place, and a **painter** is secured to the boat.

• HELMSMAN AND CREW

Keep the **bow** attached to the dolly with the **painter** while you are moving the boat around on land. Apply pressure to the bow to avoid scraping the **stern** on the ground.

• LAUNCHING DOLLY

A separate launching dolly is kinder to your boat, and saves you a great deal of trailer maintenance time. Dollies with balloon tires are designed for launching from sandy beaches.

ROAD TRAILER •

Water – especially salt water – corrodes metal, so ideally you should keep the road trailer out of the water to avoid immersing the wheel hubs and damaging the bearings.

1. Push the launching dolly into the water, with the boat's **bow** still secured to it by the **painter**.

2. When the dolly is in deep enough water, float off the boat. Do not push it off.

3. Take the dolly ashore for parking clear of the gangway, and well above the high water mark.

─────── Stage 2 ───────

FLOATING OFF

Take the dolly far enough into the water so that the boat floats clear. Don't be tempted to stop short to prevent yourself getting too wet, and try pushing the boat off – you may scratch the hull.

• CREW
Once the boat has floated off the dolly, hold it in water that is deep enough to keep it afloat, while the helmsman parks the dolly. Do not let the hull scrape against the bottom. Concrete slipways, in particular, will easily damage GRP hulls.

• BOAT
As soon as the boat starts to float clear, the wind and waves will catch it, so be ready to hold on to it and control any drift.

• HELMSMAN
Pull the dolly clear of the water, then wheel it away and park it clear of the water's edge. If space is limited on the gangway, take it back to the berth space.

RECOVERY
The process of recovering the boat from the water after sailing is exactly the reverse of launching. One person holds the boat afloat while the other fetches the dolly. Then, together, you float the boat into position on the dolly.

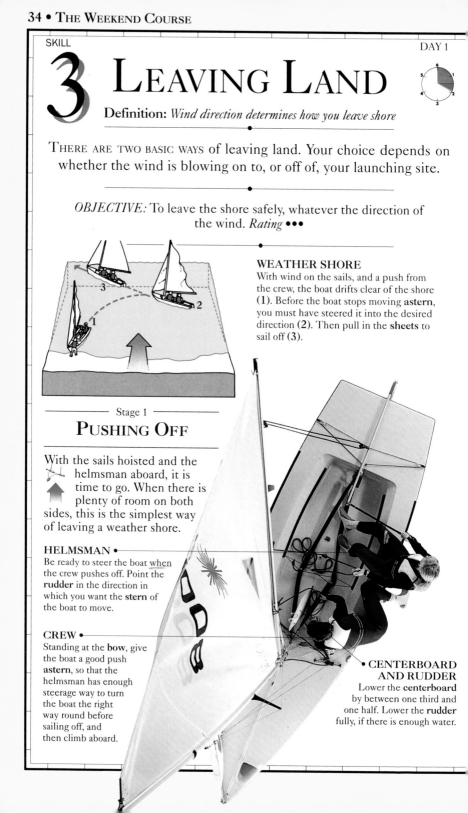

3 LEAVING LAND

Definition: *Wind direction determines how you leave shore*

THERE ARE TWO BASIC WAYS of leaving land. Your choice depends on whether the wind is blowing on to, or off of, your launching site.

OBJECTIVE: To leave the shore safely, whatever the direction of the wind. *Rating* •••

WEATHER SHORE

With wind on the sails, and a push from the crew, the boat drifts clear of the shore (**1**). Before the boat stops moving **astern**, you must have steered it into the desired direction (**2**). Then pull in the **sheets** to sail off (**3**).

Stage 1

PUSHING OFF

With the sails hoisted and the helmsman aboard, it is time to go. When there is plenty of room on both sides, this is the simplest way of leaving a weather shore.

HELMSMAN •
Be ready to steer the boat when the crew pushes off. Point the **rudder** in the direction in which you want the **stern** of the boat to move.

CREW •
Standing at the **bow**, give the boat a good push **astern**, so that the helmsman has enough steerage way to turn the boat the right way round before sailing off, and then climb aboard.

• CENTERBOARD AND RUDDER
Lower the **centerboard** by between one third and one half. Lower the **rudder** fully, if there is enough water.

Stage 3

GETTING UNDER WAY

By the time the boat stops moving **astern**, you should be pointing in your desired direction. When you have reached this stage, pull in the **sheets** to sail clear of the shore.

• TILLER
As soon as the boat stops moving **astern**, center the **tiller**. If you need to turn further away from the wind in order to clear obstacles near the shore, make sure that the **mainsheet** is slack first.

• SAIL TRIM
The **jib** used on its own will help the boat **bear away** (see p.23), so **sheet** it in first, then sheet in the **mainsail**. To **trim** the sails, ease out the sheets until the **luff** starts flapping, then pull in the sheets again until the sails stop flapping.

CREW •
Once aboard, balance the boat. For sailing away from a weather shore, particularly in light winds, this will mean moving down to **leeward** to keep the boat flat. Then **trim** the sails.

HELMSMAN •
Choose the best course to get clear of any obstructions close to the shore, and out to the sailing area. Check around inside the boat to ensure that everything is secure and tidy for the trip ahead.

ONSHORE AND OFFSHORE WINDS

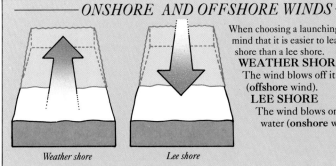

Weather shore   *Lee shore*

When choosing a launching site, bear in mind that it is easier to leave a weather shore than a lee shore.

WEATHER SHORE
The wind blows off it from the land (**offshore** wind).

LEE SHORE
The wind blows on to it from the water (**onshore** wind).

SKILL

3

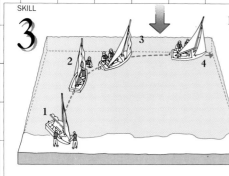

LEE SHORE

When the wind is blowing on to the shore, the **mainsail** cannot be hoisted until after the boat has been launched (1) and turned **head-to-wind** (2). If you have not already done so, attach the **rudder** and **tiller** and lower the rudder and **centerboard** as far as possible. The crew pushes the boat off as he climbs in (3) and then the helmsman chooses a course out into deeper water (4).

JIB •

Do not **sheet in** the **jib** until the boat is moving off in the right direction. Adjust the sail by pulling it in until it stops flapping.

Stage 3

PUSHING

To get some **drive** into the sails as soon as possible, the helmsman **sheets in** the **mainsail**, while the crew pushes the **bow** off in the desired direction.

• MAINSAIL

As the **mainsail** provides the majority of the **drive** needed **upwind**, and it tends to keep the **bow** up towards the wind, it should be **sheeted in** as soon as the crew starts pushing the boat.

• CREW

After pushing the boat forwards on to the desired course (see opposite), and climbing aboard, **sheet in** the **jib** and lower the **centerboard** as far as water depth allows.

•HELMSMAN

Steer a course to sail obliquely away from the shore towards deeper water.

• RUDDER AND TILLER

Although the boat can be steered satisfactorily at low speeds with only a small amount of **rudder** blade immersed, the rudder should be fully lowered as soon as possible for maximum control. If the **tiller** feels heavy, this indicates that you have forgotten to lower the rudder.

Stage 4

SAILING CLEAR

Choose a course that will take you into deep water quickly. Don't try to sail at less than about 50° to the wind until you can fully lower the **center-board** and **rudder**.

• CREW
Keep the boat sailing flat by countering the **heeling** effect with your body weight. Check that the helmsman's chosen course is not obstructed by other boats or objects in the water.

• HELMSMAN
Until you are into deep water concentrate on sail **trim** and steering a course clear of obstructions, rather than sailing as close to the wind as possible.

SAILS •
Trim the **jib** first, and then the **mainsail**, as described in Getting Underway (see p.35).

CHANGING THE ODDS

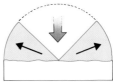

Routes for leaving a lee shore are very limited.

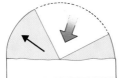

Windshifts might give one direction the advantage.

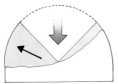

A different shape of beach shoreline may help.

LAUNCHING INTO DEEP WATER

Use this technique with an **onshore wind**. Take the boat off its trolley, point the **bow** into the wind, and hoist the sails at the water's edge (**1**). Attach the **rudder** and **tiller**. Decide in which direction to leave, then stand by what will be the boat's **windward** side. When a wave floats it, push the boat into the water, climb in (**2**), and head for deeper water. Lower the **centerboard** and rudder (**3**) to sail closer to the wind.

4 REACHING

Definition: *Sailing across the wind*

REACHING SIMPLY MEANS STEERING the boat in the desired direction, **trimming** the sails, and relaxing. On a **beam reach** the wind blows directly across the side of the boat; on a **close reach** you sail slightly closer to the wind; on a **broad reach** the wind comes from between the **beam** and the **stern**, and you sail at a broader angle to it.

OBJECTIVE: To trim the sails and balance the boat while reaching. *Rating* •

HELMSMAN •
Sit on the **windward** side. Adjust the **mainsheet** with each wind shift.

BEAM REACH

The wind is blowing directly across the side of the boat, at 90° to the **beam**.

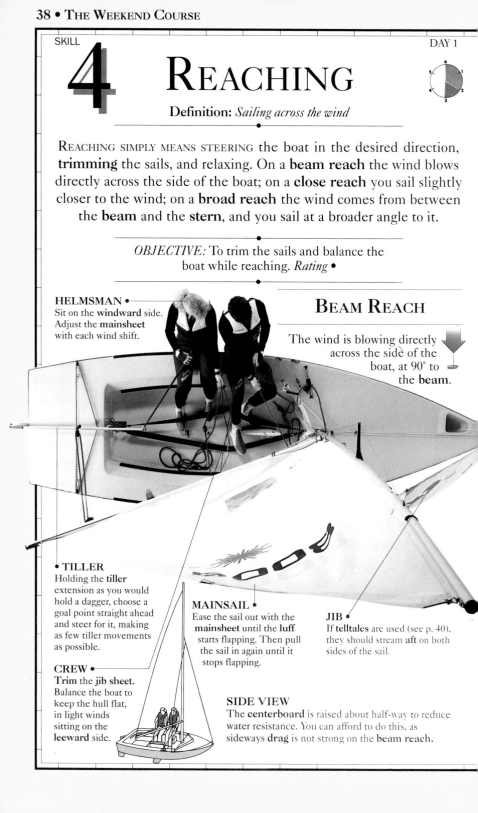

• **TILLER**
Holding the **tiller** extension as you would hold a dagger, choose a goal point straight ahead and steer for it, making as few tiller movements as possible.

CREW •
Trim the **jib sheet**. Balance the boat to keep the hull flat, in light winds sitting on the **leeward** side.

MAINSAIL •
Ease the sail out with the **mainsheet** until the **luff** starts flapping. Then pull the sail in again until it stops flapping.

JIB •
If **telltales** are used (see p. 40), they should stream **aft** on both sides of the sail.

SIDE VIEW
The **centerboard** is raised about half-way to reduce water resistance. You can afford to do this, as sideways **drag** is not strong on the beam reach.

TRIMMING THE BOAT

LEVEL HULL
The hull is most efficient when it is level. The concentrated body weight of the helmsman and crew sitting together creates less wind resistance for an easier motion.

SITTING AFT
When sailing in stronger winds, particularly **downwind**, shift your combined weight **aft** to lift the **bow** clear of the water. Do not sit too far aft, or the **stern** will **drag** in the water and slow you down.

SITTING FORWARD
In light winds, shift your combined weight slightly forward to lift the hull's flat **aft** end out of the water, reducing **drag**. If you sit too far forward, the boat will slow down.

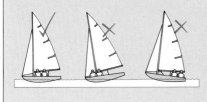

BROAD REACH

The boat is sailing with the wind coming from between the **beam** and the **stern**.

CENTERBOARD
On a beam reach there is little sideways **drag**, so raise the centerboard until it is about one third of the way down. If your boat has a **daggerboard**, do not raise it higher than the **boom**, or you will be unable to turn the boat.

• TILLER
Keep movements to a minimum while sailing a straight course. If you do want to **bear away**, ease the **mainsheet**.

• HELMSMAN
This is a relaxed point of sailing, but you should still concentrate on hull **trim**. Move **aft** if necessary to prevent the **bow** digging in.

• CREW
In medium to strong winds, sit on the **windward** side. In light winds, sit to **leeward** to balance the boat.

• JIB
Trim the sail constantly. Ease the **sheet** until the sail starts to flap or the **windward telltale** lifts, then pull it in again until the flapping stops.

• MAINSAIL
Ease the **mainsheet** as you bear away from a beam to a **broad reach**, pushing the **boom** out by hand if necessary.

CLOSE REACH

The boat is said to be on a
close reach when the wind is
at about 50°–75° to its **bow**.

• JIB
Keep an eye on the **jib
telltales** and adjust the
jib **sheet** with each
windshift.

HELMSMAN •
Concentrate on
your course and
on trimming
the **mainsail**.

• CREW
Balance the boat
and look out for
other craft.

• MAINSAIL
Wind strength and direction
rarely stay the same, so trim the
mainsail constantly. Take care not to
over-sheet, which will slow you down and
create excessive heeling.

• TILLER
Keep **tiller**
movements to a
minimum.

BACK VIEW
Notice that the centerboard
is lowered to three quarters
of its maximum extent.

TELLTALES
Telltales are strips of thick wool or cassette tape, used to
provide an accurate guide to sail trim. They are fixed a
short distance back from the **luff** of the **jib** on both sides.

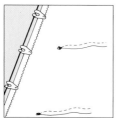

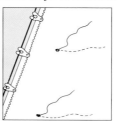

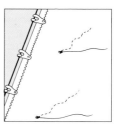

CORRECT TRIM
Both of the **telltales**
stream **aft** together.

UNDER-TRIMMING
Sheet in more when the
windward telltale lifts.

OVER-TRIMMING
Ease the **sheet** when the
leeward telltale lifts.

SHEETING IN CENTER- AND AFT-MAINSHEET RIGS

 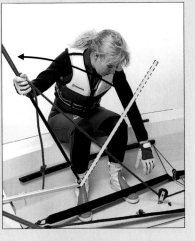

CENTER-MAINSHEET

Center-mainsheet rigging allows you to
use both hands to sheet in without having
to let go of the tiller extension.
1. Pull in as much sheet as you can with
your mainsheet hand, then swing your
tiller hand down to catch hold of the sheet.
2. Still holding the sheet and tiller
extension together in your tiller hand,
swing the extension as far **aft** as you can
without altering the position of the tiller
itself. As your tiller hand reaches the end
of its swing, reach down with your sheet
hand and take hold of the mainsheet near
the block.
3. Pull right back with your sheet hand as
far as you can, and then swing your tiller
hand back down in order to repeat the
whole process.

AFT-MAINSHEET

Hold the **tiller** in the hand that is
nearest to it, and the **mainsheet**
in the other hand.
1. Pull your sheet hand across
your body, and up to meet
your tiller hand in the final
stages of the swing.
2. Trap the mainsheet under
the thumb of your tiller
hand. This frees your sheet
hand to regain hold of the
sheet. Repeat the process.

5 TACKING

Definition: *Turning the boat around through the wind.*

THIS BASIC TURNING MANEUVER is achieved by **luffing up** (altering course into the wind) until the **bow** points directly at the wind, and then continuing the turn until the wind drives the sails on the other side. It can be broken down into the seven stages that are illustrated in sequence over the next four pages. During the turn, the helmsman crosses from one side of the boat to the other, and must change hands on the **tiller** and **mainsheet** while steering through the complete maneuver, so it is worth practicing the technique in the boat before going afloat. Any initial problems can be solved, then, in safety.

OBJECTIVE: To turn the boat from a **beam reach** on one **tack** to the beam reach on the opposite tack, coordinating the actions of helmsman and crew. *Rating* •••

1: SAILING ON A BEAM REACH
Keep the hull of the boat flat and the sails **trimmed** to ensure your maximum speed.

2: CHECKING THE HORIZON
The helmsman warns the crew of the maneuver by saying "Ready About". The crew then checks the area into which the boat will turn and, if all is clear, replies "Ready".

3: INITIATING THE TURN
As the helmsman calls "Hard–a–lee" and pushes the **tiller** to **leeward** to start the turn, the crew releases the **jib sheet** (see opposite).

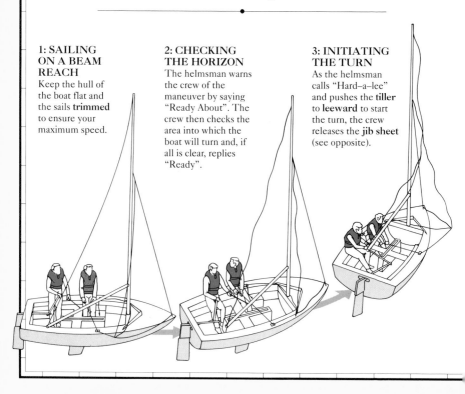

TACKING HINTS

BE PATIENT
The whole maneuver takes much longer than you might anticipate.

SHEETING THE JIB
The crew must not **sheet in** the **jib** on the new side until the sail has blown across to the new **leeward** side of the boat.

CHANGING SIDES
The helmsman must not be too eager to cross to the new **windward** side. Wait until the **boom** reaches the center of the boat.

CONTINUE TO STEER
The helmsman straightens the **tiller** only when the boat is on the new course.

Stage 3

INITIATING THE TURN

At this stage the helmsman must remember to face forward when turning the boat, and to change hands on the **tiller** and **mainsheet** only after the **tack** is complete.

• JIB
The **jib** is released to aid the turn into the wind.

MAINSAIL •
As the power is lost, the **mainsail** starts to flap.

CREW •
Release the **jib sheet** and be ready to move across the boat. Have the new jib sheet to hand, but do not pull it in yet.

• CENTER-BOARD
When turning from one **reach** to another, keep the **centerboard** half-lowered.

• TILLER
Push the **tiller** extension over with a firm movement until the **rudder** is at about 30° to the centerline. Keep it there until the turn is complete.

• HELMSMAN
Call "Hard–a–lee" to warn the crew that you have pushed the **tiller** to **leeward**. You must face forwards when turning, so be ready with your back foot across the boat, but wait until the **boom** swings towards you before starting to move.

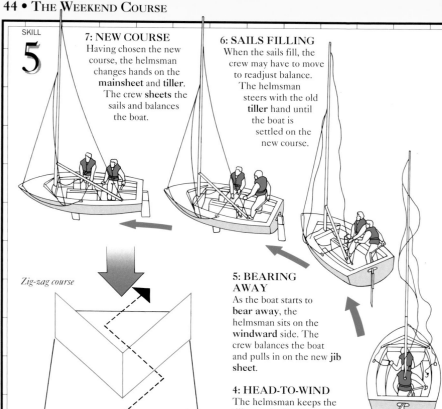

7: NEW COURSE
Having chosen the new course, the helmsman changes hands on the **mainsheet** and **tiller**. The crew **sheets** the sails and balances the boat.

6: SAILS FILLING
When the sails fill, the crew may have to move to readjust balance. The helmsman steers with the old **tiller** hand until the boat is settled on the new course.

Zig-zag course

5: BEARING AWAY
As the boat starts to **bear away**, the helmsman sits on the **windward** side. The crew balances the boat and pulls in on the new **jib sheet**.

4: HEAD-TO-WIND
The helmsman keeps the **tiller** pushed over as the boat passes through the **head-to-wind** position on to the new **tack**. The crew waits for the **jib** to cross on to the new **leeward** side, then pulls in the new **jib sheet**.

ACHIEVING A WINDWARD GOAL
Tacking is a basic part of sailing to **windward** as well as a turning maneuver. The efficient way of reaching a windward goal is by following a zig-zag course (marked by the broken line) and tacking between each leg.

HELMSMAN'S ACTIONS

1. Initiate the **tack** by pushing the **tiller** extension away.
2. When the **boom** swings across, move to the other side. Facing forwards, lead with the tiller hand and swivel on the balls of your feet.
3. Steer on to the new course. Bring the **sheet** hand back to grasp the tiller extension, still holding the **mainsheet**.
4. Grasp the sheet with the old tiller hand, then bring the tiller extension around to your front.

1

2

Stage 7

SETTING A NEW COURSE

The boat has now turned right through the wind. The helmsman and crew must both be ready to sail a new course, balancing the boat and **trimming** the sails.

• CREW
Sit in a position that balances the boat and watch the **telltales** to **sheet** the **jib** for the new course. Set the jib as soon as possible, as it influences the airflow over the **mainsail**.

• HELMSMAN
Steer with the old **tiller** hand until the boat has settled on to the new course, then change hands on the tiller and **mainsheet**.

CENTERBOARD •
Leave the position of the **centerboard** unaltered through the tack, then adjust it for the new course.

3

4

• TILLER
Once the boat is settled on the new course, keep **tiller** movements to a minimum to reduce **drag**.

• MAINSAIL
After a **tack** from a **beam reach** on to another reach, the helmsman should **sheet in** the **mainsail** until the **luff** stops flapping.

SKILL

5 TACKING OPTION

Almost all international small boat classes are **rigged** center-mainsheet, with the **mainsheet** in the center of the **boom**. Hundreds of other classes, particularly in the UK, have the more traditional **aft-mainsheet** system. The techniques for **tacking** and **jibing** these boats differ in two respects: the helmsman changes hands on **tiller** and **mainsheet** before the maneuver, rather than at the end; and the helmsman faces **aft** when crossing the boat. The action of the crew is the same as for center-mainsheet tacking.

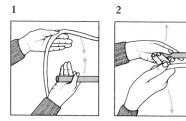

1   2

3: BEARING AWAY
After the **tack**, the helmsman continues to **bear away** until the desired new course is reached, then both helmsman and crew trim the sails by **sheeting** them in until they stop flapping. The **centerboard** is then adjusted for the new course.

CHANGING HANDS
Change hands before the **tacking** maneuver by bringing the **tiller** extension and **mainsheet** together. **1.** Hold each between thumb and forefinger of the respective hands. Keep the palms open. **2.** Put the mainsheet into the tiller hand and then bring the old mainsheet hand away again, this time holding the tiller.

2: HEAD TO WIND
As the **boom** swings over the centerline, the helmsman crosses the boat, facing **aft**. Note that she still holds the **tiller** over to keep the boat turning. The crew also crosses to the new side (see opposite).

1: INITIATING THE TURN
The helmsman checks that the area into which she will sail is clear, calls "Ready About" to warn the crew, then changes hands on the **tiller** extension and **mainsheet**. With front foot forwards, ready for the turn, she initiates the **tack** by pushing the tiller extension away and holding it in place.

Stage 2

HEAD TO WIND

At the mid-point of the maneuver there is no **drive** in the sails, but the boat is still turning. In aft-mainsheet tacking, the helmsman faces **aft** throughout the turn, so it is vital to check the surrounding area before **tacking**.

JIB •
The **jib** flaps idly at this stage, and will cross to the new **leeward** side of its own accord. Do not try to **sheet in** too early, or you might turn the **bow** back towards the original course.

MAINSAIL •
The **mainsail** crosses slowly to the new **leeward** side as the boat passes through the **head-to-wind** position.

CREW •
Move from one side of the boat to the other, taking the new **jib sheet** with you, ready to **sheet in** after the helmsman has borne away on to the new course.

HELMSMAN •
As the **boom** swings across, cross to the new **windward** side, leading with the front foot and swiveling on the balls of both feet.

CENTERBOARD
Leave the **centerboard** down throughout the maneuver, so that it acts as the pivot point about which the boat turns.

TILLER •
It is important to keep the tiller extension held over throughout the tack, until the boat has assumed the correct new course.

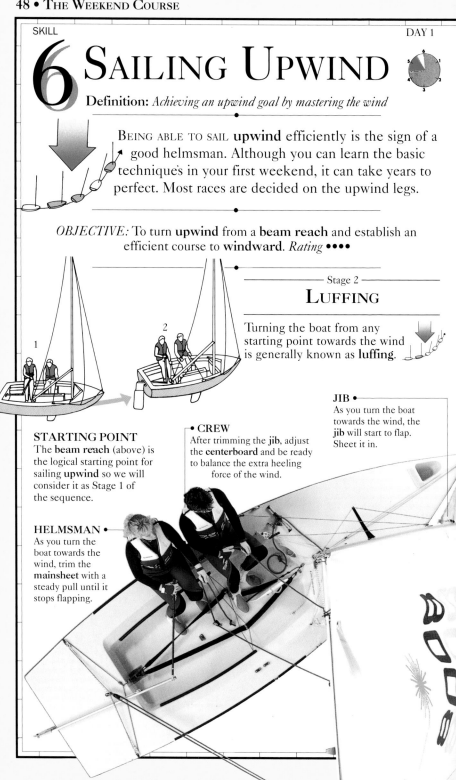

6 SAILING UPWIND

Definition: *Achieving an upwind goal by mastering the wind*

BEING ABLE TO SAIL **upwind** efficiently is the sign of a good helmsman. Although you can learn the basic techniques in your first weekend, it can take years to perfect. Most races are decided on the upwind legs.

OBJECTIVE: To turn **upwind** from a **beam reach** and establish an efficient course to **windward**. *Rating* ••••

——— Stage 2 ———

LUFFING

Turning the boat from any starting point towards the wind is generally known as **luffing**.

JIB •
As you turn the boat towards the wind, the **jib** will start to flap. Sheet it in.

• CREW
After trimming the **jib**, adjust the **centerboard** and be ready to balance the extra heeling force of the wind.

STARTING POINT
The **beam reach** (above) is the logical starting point for sailing **upwind** so we will consider it as Stage 1 of the sequence.

HELMSMAN •
As you turn the boat towards the wind, trim the **mainsheet** with a steady pull until it stops flapping.

Stage 3

CLOSE REACH

When the boat is at about 60°–70° to the wind, it is in **close reach** – you are starting to sail to **windward**.

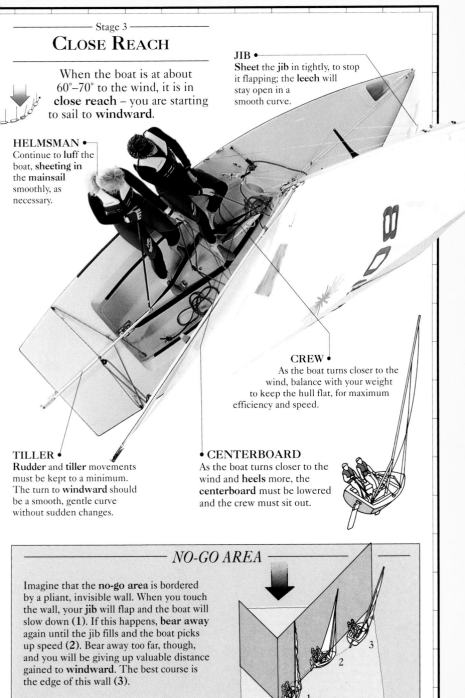

JIB •
Sheet the **jib** in tightly, to stop it flapping; the **leech** will stay open in a smooth curve.

HELMSMAN •
Continue to luff the boat, **sheeting in** the **mainsail** smoothly, as necessary.

CREW •
As the boat turns closer to the wind, balance with your weight to keep the hull flat, for maximum efficiency and speed.

TILLER •
Rudder and **tiller** movements must be kept to a minimum. The turn to **windward** should be a smooth, gentle curve without sudden changes.

• CENTERBOARD
As the boat turns closer to the wind and **heels** more, the **centerboard** must be lowered and the crew must sit out.

NO-GO AREA

Imagine that the **no-go area** is bordered by a pliant, invisible wall. When you touch the wall, your **jib** will flap and the boat will slow down (**1**). If this happens, **bear away** again until the jib fills and the boat picks up speed (**2**). Bear away too far, though, and you will be giving up valuable distance gained to **windward**. The best course is the edge of this wall (**3**).

SKILL

6

HEAVING-TO

The controlled way of stopping when afloat,
without actually lowering the sails, is to **heave-to**
– the drive of the **jib** and the action of the **rudder**
counteract each other, and reduce speed. Achieve
this by **tacking** without freeing the jibsheet.

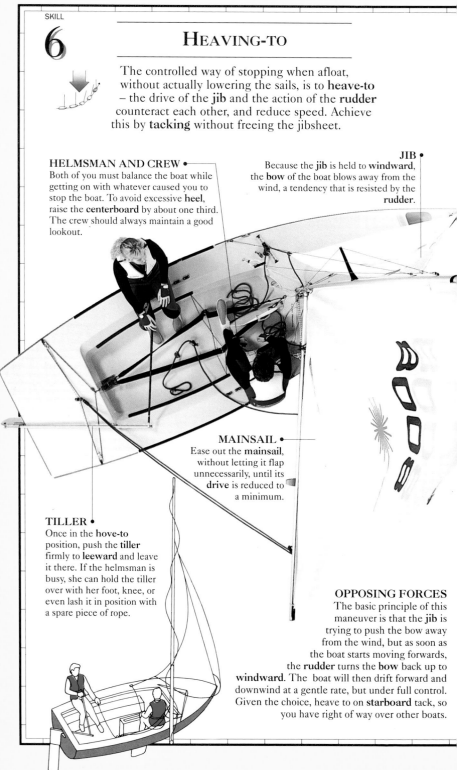

HELMSMAN AND CREW •
Both of you must balance the boat while
getting on with whatever caused you to
stop the boat. To avoid excessive **heel**,
raise the **centerboard** by about one third.
The crew should always maintain a good
lookout.

JIB •
Because the **jib** is held to **windward**,
the **bow** of the boat blows away from the
wind, a tendency that is resisted by the
rudder.

MAINSAIL •
Ease out the **mainsail**,
without letting it flap
unnecessarily, until its
drive is reduced to
a minimum.

TILLER •
Once in the **hove-to**
position, push the **tiller**
firmly to **leeward** and leave
it there. If the helmsman is
busy, she can hold the tiller
over with her foot, knee, or
even lash it in position with
a spare piece of rope.

OPPOSING FORCES
The basic principle of this
maneuver is that the **jib** is
trying to push the bow away
from the wind, but as soon as
the boat starts moving forwards,
the **rudder** turns the **bow** back up to
windward. The boat will then drift forward and
downwind at a gentle rate, but under full control.
Given the choice, heave to on **starboard** tack, so
you have right of way over other boats.

STARTING AND STOPPING

HEAVING-TO

Heaving-to is the best way of stopping for a short time when afloat. The boat remains in full control and is ready to sail away again almost instantly. There are 2 other ways of stopping which may be preferable in certain circumstances.

LYING-TO

This is a good way of stopping for a few moments, perhaps to change over positions in the boat. Head on a **close reach** and let out both **sheets** completely. If you try doing it with the boat on anything more than a **close reach**, the sails cannot be let far enough out to stop the boat.

HEAD-TO-WIND

Turn the boat **head-to-wind** so that all **drive** is removed from the sails. As soon as it has stopped moving forwards, the boat will be blown **astern** by the windage of the flapping sails and will turn following the direction of the **rudder**.

MOVING AWAY

Sailing away from the hove-to position is straightforward: simply **sheet** the **jib** in on the **leeward** side, sheet in the **mainsail,** and straighten the **tiller**.

7 RETURNING TO LAND

Definition: *The approach varies according to wind direction*

THE TECHNIQUES USED FOR RETURNING TO A BEACH (see pp.52–53) and for returning to a pontoon (see pp.54–55) are different from each other, and depend on whether the wind is **onshore** or **offshore**.

OBJECTIVE: To learn how to return safely to land in different weather conditions. *Rating* •••

RETURNING TO A BEACH

You can sail directly on to the shore only when the wind blows parallel to it. Sailing on to a lee shore, or a weather shore, is less straightforward.

LEE SHORE
A For a safe approach turn **head-to-wind (1)**, drop the **mainsail**, and come in **(2)** under the **jib** . **B** Or sail into shallow water on a **broad reach (1)**, turn **head-to-wind (2)**, get out, lower the sails, turn the boat **(3)** and pull it ashore.

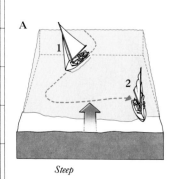

Steep

Shallow

WEATHER SHORE
A. If the shore shelves steeply, **tack** in **(1)**, and reach along the shore to your chosen landing spot. Turn **head-to-wind (2)**, get out, and lower the sails. **B.** In shallow water, tack in **(1)**, raising the **centerboard** in good time, until you reach the shore **(2)**.

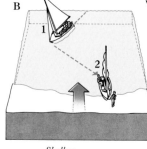

LEE SHORE APPROACH

The helmsman chose the safe option (**A, 2**). The **mainsail** has been lowered, so the final approach was under **jib** alone.

• HELMSMAN
Remove the **rudder** and **tiller** to avoid possible damage before the boat is brought ashore.

RUDDER •
When landing in shallow water, lift up the blade by hand as you approach the shore, but before you reach it.

CREW •
Hold the boat clear of the bottom to avoid damaging the hull through contact with the beach or gangway.

MAINSAIL •
Stow away the **mainsail** once ashore. Make sure the **boom** does not obstruct the **tiller**.

CENTERBOARD
The **centerboard** should have been raised entirely as you were coming ashore. Double-check that it is raised before putting the boat on to its dolly.

JIB •
To prevent it flapping, either furl the **jib** by rolling it around itself and securing it with one of the jib **sheets**, or lower it completely.

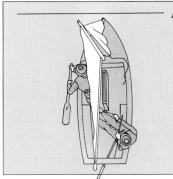

PADDLING

ONE PADDLE
With 1 paddle, the crew sits just behind the **shroud** to paddle, while the helmsman sits on the other side, and uses the **rudder** to counter the effect of the paddle. If only one person is aboard, kneel at the **stern** and paddle the boat stern first.

TWO PADDLES
With 2 paddles, both helmsman and crew can paddle, sitting just behind the **shrouds**.

7

RETURNING TO A DOCK

Landing at a dock or jetty is slightly trickier than landing on the shore. The object at which you are aiming is smaller, so you have to control your speed of approach more precisely. The techniques, however, are similar to those for returning to the beach (see pp.52–53), although you may have to take account of a strong tide running past the dock.

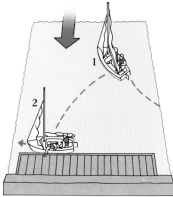

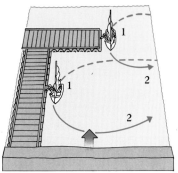

LEE SHORE

If the dock is parallel to the shore, sail **head-to-wind** well clear of the dock and lower the **mainsail (1)**. Come alongside under **jib** alone, letting it flap, so the boat drifts gently **(2)**.

WEATHER SHORE

Approach on a **close reach**, letting the sails out as you near the dock. Turn up **head-to-wind** to stop alongside **(1)**. Plan your escape route **(2)** so that you are ready to leave again in due course.

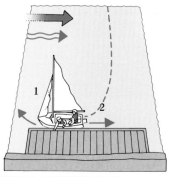

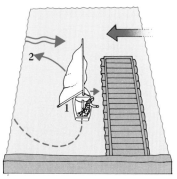

TIDAL CONDITIONS

When tide (wavy arrow) and wind are together, approach on a **reach**, and make the final turn into both wind and tide **(1)**. Try to judge how much you are being set down by the tide and allow for this by heading further up wind and tide. Secure the boat as soon as you are alongside **(2)**.

OPPOSING TIDE AND WIND

When the tide is running in the opposite direction to which the wind is blowing, approach the dock on its **leeward** side **(1)**. Let the sails flap so that the boat drifts in with the tide, which is likely to be slack near the shore. Sail away again by **sheeting in** and **bearing away (2)**.

• DOCK
The wind rarely blows in line with the dock. Make your approach on the side that is to **leeward**.

•CREW
With the **painter** in your hand, hold on to the dock ready to climb out and secure the boat.

AT THE DOCK

If possible, approach on the **leeward** side, so that the wind blows you away from the shore.

• MAINSAIL
By approaching on the **leeward** side, the **mainsail** flaps away from the dock, keeping the boat clear and leaving the crew more room to move about.

• HELMSMAN
Balance the boat while the crew secures it, then lower the sails and remove the **rudder**.

RUDDER •
If the water close to the shore is shallow, raise the **rudder** blade partially before approaching the dock to avoid causing any damage to it.

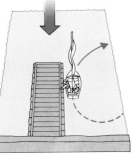

DOCK APPROACH
Come in on a **broad reach**, then turn **head-to-wind** alongside.

WEATHER SHORE PONTOON

The order of tasks is slightly different from those outlined for a lee shore dock.

• Secure the **painter** to the dock **cleat** or mooring line with a round turn and 2 half hitches (see p.14).

• Raise the **centerboard** fully. Alternatively, if your boat has a **daggerboard**, remove it from the case completely and secure it in the boat.

• Lower the **mainsail**, roll it neatly, and secure it with the end of the **mainsheet**.

• Remove the **rudder** and **tiller**.

• Roll up the **jib** and secure it to the **forestay** with the jib **sheets**. Alternatively, lower it completely.

• Put out your own fender to protect the boat if the dock is not well buffered.

SKILL

DAY 2

8 SAILING DOWNWIND

Definition: *Sailing with the wind behind the boat*

WHEN SAILING **downwind**, it is tempting just to sit and relax. The sails push the boat forward, there is no **leeway** to worry about, and the boat feels stable. To get the most out of your performance, however, you must pay as much attention to sail and boat **trim** as when you're sailing **upwind**.

OBJECTIVE: To learn how to **bear away** when sailing on a **beam reach**, and then sail **downwind**. *Rating* ••

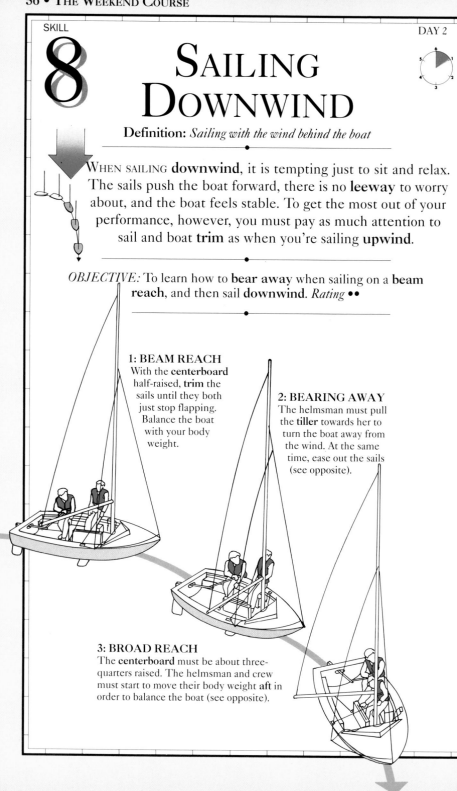

1: BEAM REACH
With the **centerboard** half-raised, **trim** the sails until they both just stop flapping. Balance the boat with your body weight.

2: BEARING AWAY
The helmsman must pull the **tiller** towards her to turn the boat away from the wind. At the same time, ease out the sails (see opposite).

3: BROAD REACH
The **centerboard** must be about three-quarters raised. The helmsman and crew must start to move their body weight **aft** in order to balance the boat (see opposite).

HOW TO BEAR AWAY

To **bear away** from the wind, pull the **tiller** towards you, and ease out the **mainsheet**. The **mainsail** tries to turn the boat up towards the wind, so do not fight against it with the **rudder**. If you bear away in a strong wind without easing the mainsheet, you could break the tiller. Also consider boat **heel**. Have the boat flat or heeled slightly to **windward**. One control is set against the other if you bear away when the boat is heeled to **leeward**.

Stage 3

BROAD REACH

On a **broad reach**, you have borne away so that the wind is blowing obliquely over the **stern** of the boat.

• TILLER
Keep the **tiller** and **rudder** in a straight line, with minimum movement to reduce **drag**.

• HELMSMAN
Move **aft** to keep the boat **trimmed** flat, and concentrate on sail setting. The wind is coming from over your shoulder, so watch **astern** occasionally for gusts.

• CREW
In strong winds, sit to **windward** to balance the boat. In light winds, move down and sit to **leeward** so that the helmsman can sit out for a better view and greater control.

• CENTERBOARD
The **centerboard** must be about three-quarters raised, as there is little sideways **drag**. If the boat has a **daggerboard**, do not raise it above the level of the **boom**.

SAILS •
When you were **bearing away**, you eased out the sails, then pulled them in again until they just stopped flapping. If the **jib fairleads** are adjustable, move them out and back for greater efficiency.

SKILL

8

--- Stage 4 ---

TRAINING RUN

When **running** dead **downwind**, a windshift or change of course can bring the wind behind the **mainsail** so that the **boom** swings across the boat unexpectedly. Sailing downwind on a training run prevents this from occurring.

• TILLER
Keep an eye on the water flow leaving the **rudder**; if it becomes very turbulent, you may be sitting too far **aft**.

HELMSMAN •
Usually you sit to **windward** for maximum control and a good view. Watch your course carefully.

MAINSAIL •
The **mainsail** is right out against the **leeward** shroud. In light winds, you might need to hold the **boom** out there.

CREW •
Sit down to **leeward** and, if necessary, in light winds hold the **boom** out with one hand. From this position, you can watch to leeward for other boats.

JIB •
As it is blanketed by the **mainsail**, the **jib** goes dead. If it tries to blow across to set on the **windward** side, the helmsman must **luff** very gently until it returns to the **leeward** side.

CENTERBOARD
Have the **centerboard** almost fully raised, leaving just a small amount down to provide grip on the water. If your boat has a **daggerboard**, do not raise the board to a level higher than that of the **boom**.

MAINTAINING SPEED

• Keep the boat balanced and **trimmed** flat **fore** and **aft**. Except in very light winds, aim to get your weight aft to stop the **bow** burying itself in the waves ahead.

• As you **bear away** to sail **downwind**, the **centerboard** is raised. Lower it when you start to sail **upwind** again, otherwise you will find yourself drifting sideways.

Stage 5

GOOSE-WINGED

If you **bear away** further, the **jib** will blow across to the **windward** side and fill, clear of the influence of the **mainsail**. At this point, the wind is blowing directly from **astern**, and the boat is running **goose-winged**.

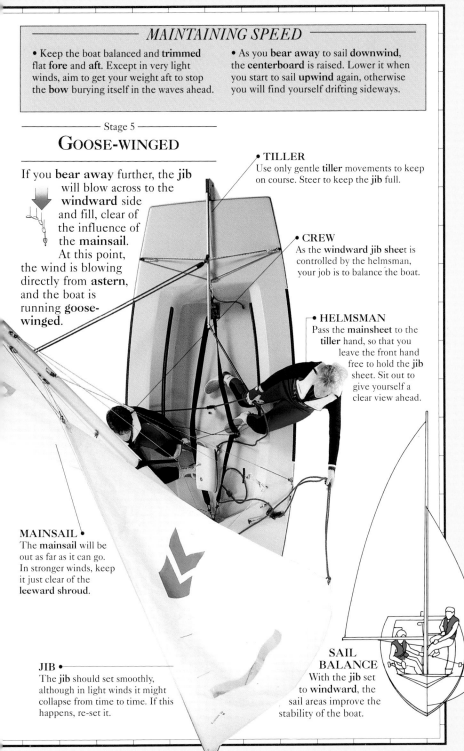

TILLER
Use only gentle **tiller** movements to keep on course. Steer to keep the **jib** full.

CREW
As the **windward jib sheet** is controlled by the helmsman, your job is to balance the boat.

HELMSMAN
Pass the **mainsheet** to the **tiller** hand, so that you leave the front hand free to hold the **jib** sheet. Sit out to give yourself a clear view ahead.

MAINSAIL
The **mainsail** will be out as far as it can go. In stronger winds, keep it just clear of the **leeward shroud**.

JIB
The **jib** should set smoothly, although in light winds it might collapse from time to time. If this happens, re-set it.

SAIL BALANCE
With the **jib** set to **windward**, the sail areas improve the stability of the boat.

JIBING

Definition: *Turning the stern of the boat through the wind*

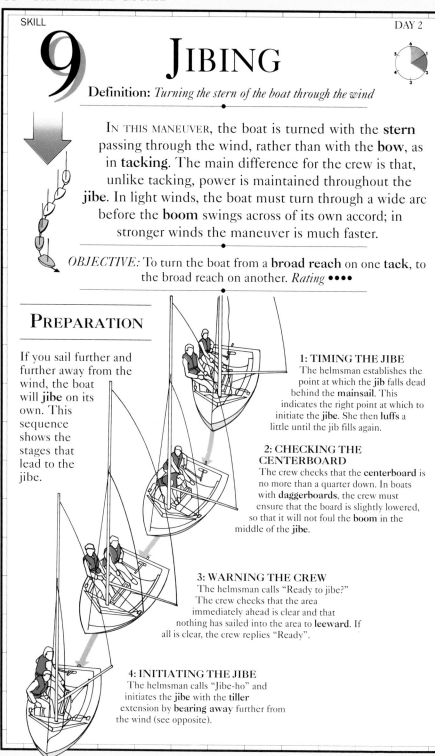

IN THIS MANEUVER, the boat is turned with the **stern** passing through the wind, rather than with the **bow**, as in **tacking**. The main difference for the crew is that, unlike tacking, power is maintained throughout the **jibe**. In light winds, the boat must turn through a wide arc before the **boom** swings across of its own accord; in stronger winds the maneuver is much faster.

OBJECTIVE: To turn the boat from a **broad reach** on one **tack**, to the broad reach on another. *Rating* ••••

PREPARATION

If you sail further and further away from the wind, the boat will **jibe** on its own. This sequence shows the stages that lead to the jibe.

1: TIMING THE JIBE
The helmsman establishes the point at which the **jib** falls dead behind the **mainsail**. This indicates the right point at which to initiate the **jibe**. She then **luffs** a little until the jib fills again.

2: CHECKING THE CENTERBOARD
The crew checks that the **centerboard** is no more than a quarter down. In boats with **daggerboards**, the crew must ensure that the board is slightly lowered, so that it will not foul the **boom** in the middle of the **jibe**.

3: WARNING THE CREW
The helmsman calls "Ready to jibe?" The crew checks that the area immediately ahead is clear and that nothing has sailed into the area to **leeward**. If all is clear, the crew replies "Ready".

4: INITIATING THE JIBE
The helmsman calls "Jibe-ho" and initiates the **jibe** with the **tiller** extension by **bearing away** further from the wind (see opposite).

TILLER •
Hold the **tiller** over firmly as the boat goes into the **jibe**, but be ready to center it again as the **boom** crosses the centerline of the boat.

Stage 4
INITIATING THE JIBE

The actions are the same, in principle, as for **tacking** (see pp.42–45), except that the helmsman pulls the **tiller** towards her.

• HELMSMAN
Pull the **tiller** extension firmly to take the boat through the **jibe**. Grasp the **mainsheet** from either the **block** or the falls.

• CREW
Balance the boat throughout the **jibe**. In light winds, sit down to **leeward** before the jibe, and be ready to move across the boat.

MAINSAIL •
The mainsail gives a clear indication of when the **boom** is about to swing across. Watch the **clew** (trailing edge) about one third of the way up and you will see it fold to **windward** as the wind starts to blow on the other side of the sail and pushes the boom across.

• JIB
The **jib** moves across of its own accord, and can be kept full almost all the way through the maneuver.

CENTERBOARD
The less **centerboard** that protrudes beneath the boat, the less likely the boat is to trip over it in the **jibe**.

Stage 5

MID-JIBE

Halfway through the **jibe**, the **boom** swings across the boat towards the new **leeward** side. For a few seconds the boom, helmsman, and **tiller** are all in a straight line before the sail fills again.

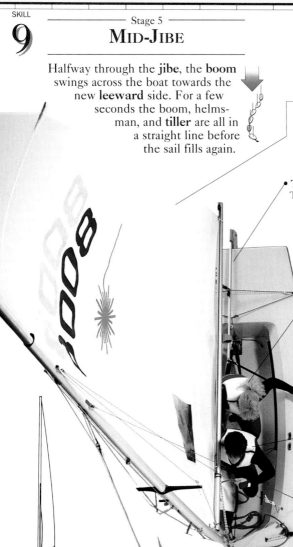

• MAINSAIL
As the **mainsail** swings across, it loses its **drive** for only a very short time. As soon as it fills again on the new side, the boat will start to accelerate.

• TILLER
The **tiller** must be central as the **boom** swings across. If it is not, the boat will attempt to turn up towards the wind as soon as the **mainsail** fills. In strong winds this can be quite dramatic.

• HELMSMAN
As the **boom** starts to swing across, move into the center of the boat, facing forwards and leading with the back foot. Keep below the level of the boom, and remember to center the **tiller** as the boom reaches the centerline of the boat.

• CREW
Balance the boat as necessary, keeping your head below the level of the **boom**. Do not free off the old **jib sheet** too soon, but take hold of the new jib sheet and be ready to **trim** it.

• JIB
As the **boom** swings across, the **jib** may fill again on the old side. Having been blanketed by the **mainsail**, it is now in clear air again.

FRONT VIEW
When the boat is pointing directly **downwind**, both helmsman and crew are at the boat's center, waiting for power to return as the sails fill again.

Stage 6

SETTING A NEW COURSE

In the final stage, the helmsman steers the boat on to the new course before changing hands on the **tiller** and **mainsheet**. The crew balances the boat by sitting to **leeward** in light winds (see photograph), and to **windward** in stronger winds (see illustration).

• HELMSMAN
Steer on to the new course with the old **tiller** hand. Wait until the boat is settled before changing hands and **mainsheet**, as for tacking (see pp.44–45).

• CREW
In light winds, sit to **leeward**, **trim** the **jib** for the new course, and adjust the **centerboard** according to your point of sailing. Check that the way ahead is clear.

• MAINSAIL
After the **boom** reaches the new side, the **mainsail** fills at once. **Trim** it for the new course as soon as the helmsman has changed hands on **mainsheet** and **tiller**.

STAYING LEVEL
In stronger winds, the crew moves to **windward** to keep the boat level. Once the **jibe** is completed, they can adjust sail **trim**, **centerboard**, and the balance.

• JIB
A common mistake is to **sheet in** the **jib** too tightly after the **jibe**, particularly if you are sailing off on another **broad reach**. Use the **telltales** as an accurate guide to jib **trim**.

SKILL

9 JIBING OPTION

There is one main obstacle to **jibing** boats that are rigged aft-mainsheet, and this is that the helmsman faces away from the direction of travel throughout the most critical part of the maneuver – while the boat is turning. For this reason, the time spent completing the jibe should be kept to a minimum. It is also vital to make an accurate assessment of the distance the boat will cover during the jibe, and for the crew to check that the area surrounding the boat is clear.

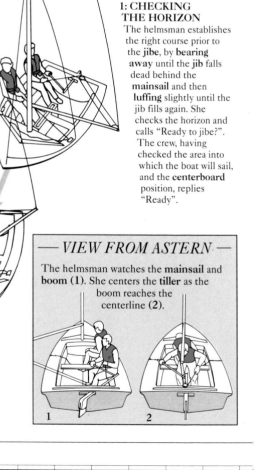

1: CHECKING THE HORIZON

The helmsman establishes the right course prior to the **jibe**, by **bearing away** until the **jib** falls dead behind the **mainsail** and then **luffing** slightly until the jib fills again. She checks the horizon and calls "Ready to jibe?". The crew, having checked the area into which the boat will sail, and the **centerboard** position, replies "Ready".

2: INITIATING THE JIBE

The helmsman changes hands on the **mainsheet** and **tiller** extension, calls "Jibe-ho", and initiates the **jibe** by pushing the tiller extension to the **windward** side. She watches the **leech** of the **mainsail** to see when the boom will swing across, and prepares to cross the boat.

3: MID-JIBE

As the **boom** swings across, the helmsman faces **aft** in the center of the boat. The moment the boom crosses the centerline, she centers the **tiller**. The crew waits to move to either side. He holds the new **jib sheet**, ready to **sheet in** on the new course (see opposite).

VIEW FROM ASTERN

The helmsman watches the **mainsail** and **boom** (1). She centers the **tiller** as the boom reaches the centerline (2).

1

2

— Stage 3 —
MID-JIBE

Compare the mid-point in the maneuver with Stage 5 for the center-mainsheet boat (see p62). The principal differences are that here the helmsman faces **aft**, and that she has already changed hands on the **mainsheet** and **tiller** extension.

HELMSMAN •
Move to the center of the boat, facing **aft**, just before the **boom** reaches the centerline. Center the **tiller** when the boom reaches the centerline, in preparation for when the **drive** comes on to the **mainsail** again.

MAINSAIL •
As the **boom** swings across, a large loop of **mainsheet** crosses the boat's **stern**. It may get caught on the corner of the **transom**, so be ready to free it.

CREW •
Balance the boat after the **jibe** by moving from the center of the boat to either the new **windward** or **leeward** side, depending on the wind strength and the intended new course.

JIB •
The **jib** moves across to the new **leeward** side on its own, but the crew must have the new **jib sheet** ready in order to **trim** the sail as soon as the new course is set.

CENTERBOARD
Only a little **centerboard** is needed – just enough to give the boat some grip on the water. Too much centerboard will make the **jibe** more violent and you could capsize when the power comes on to the sails again.

SKILL

DAY 2

10 SAILING A FULL CIRCLE

Definition: *To sail in a full circle efficiently, you have to use all the techniques you have learned during the weekend course*

BY THIS STAGE, you are familiar with the techniques for sailing in every direction, except into the **no-go area** which extends at an angle of approximately 45° on either side of the wind direction. In this skill you learn how to merge these individual maneuvers in order to progress smoothly and efficiently from one point of sailing to the next.

OBJECTIVE: To put all previously learned boat-handling techniques into practice. *Rating* •••••

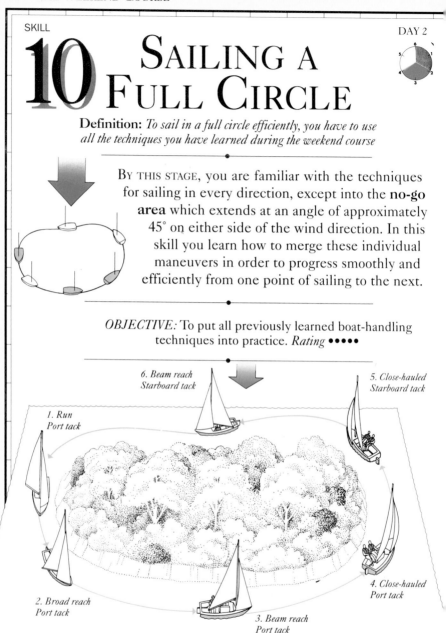

6. Beam reach
Starboard tack

5. Close-hauled
Starboard tack

1. Run
Port tack

2. Broad reach
Port tack

3. Beam reach
Port tack

4. Close-hauled
Port tack

CIRCULAR COURSE

In the diagram above, we have shown the boat sailing on a course that takes it around an island, but any simple object – for example, a marker buoy – is adequate. When you are learning how to sail a full circle, and, the first few times that you practice the maneuver, it is best to choose a stretch of open water, unpopulated by other craft, and sail around an imaginary object. Then, if the maneuver does not go according to plan, there will be no obstacles in the way.

Stage 1

JIBING ON A RUN

In order to sail a full circle, you will have to **jibe** about halfway down your intended **downwind** leg. After the jibe, bring the boat under control on a **run** before **luffing up** towards a **broad reach**, and then a **beam reach**.

• MAINSAIL
The sail is out against the **shroud**. **Sheet in** gradually as you **luff** towards a **reach**, keeping the sail full, without sheeting it too tightly.

• RUDDER
Remember that the **rudder** acts as a brake whenever its position is not straight. All **tiller** movements must be smooth and positive.

• HELMSMAN
After the **jibe**, glance **astern** occasionallly to make sure that the boat is **trimmed** correctly. If there is much turbulence left by the passage of the boat, your weight is balanced too far **aft**.

CREW •
When **running**, sit to **leeward**. Move into the center of the boat and then to **windward** to keep the boat balanced and flat when the helmsman **luffs up**.

JIB •
During the **jibe**, the **jib** crosses the boat of its own accord. Watch the **telltales** and **trim** the jib accordingly.

CENTERBOARD •
When **running**, have the **centerboard** almost fully raised. With a **daggerboard**, the board must be kept just below the level of the **boom** prior to the **jibe**.

SKILL

10

BEAM REACH

Turning through 90°, the boat has been **luffed** from a **run** to a **beam reach**. The helmsman and crew have reacted to the change of course by **trimming** the sails, adjusting the **centerboard**, and moving their weight.

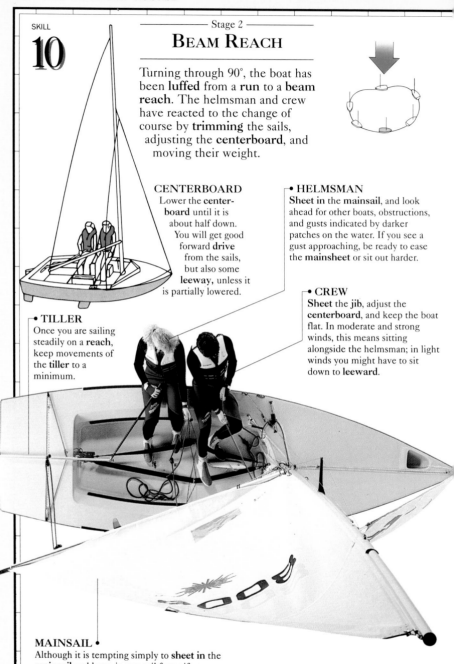

CENTERBOARD
Lower the **center-board** until it is about half down. You will get good forward **drive** from the sails, but also some **leeway,** unless it is partially lowered.

• HELMSMAN
Sheet in the **mainsail**, and look ahead for other boats, obstructions, and gusts indicated by darker patches on the water. If you see a gust approaching, be ready to ease the **mainsheet** or sit out harder.

• TILLER
Once you are sailing steadily on a **reach**, keep movements of the **tiller** to a minimum.

• CREW
Sheet the **jib**, adjust the **centerboard**, and keep the boat flat. In moderate and strong winds, this means sitting alongside the helmsman; in light winds you might have to sit down to **leeward**.

MAINSAIL •
Although it is tempting simply to **sheet in** the **mainsail** and leave it, you sail faster if you pay continuous attention to sail **trim**. The wind is rarely steady, either in strength or direction, particularly on inland waters.

Stage 3

CLOSE-HAULED

When you are sailing **close-hauled**, the sails are fully **sheeted in**, and the helmsman steers the boat according to the wind, rather than aiming in the desired direction and adjusting the sails as necessary.

• HELMSMAN AND CREW
For efficient sailing, keep the boat flat. Sit close together to minimize wind resistance on your bodies.

CENTER-BOARD •
Fully lower the **centerboard** for maximum resistance to **leeway**.

• JIB
The crew must **sheet in** the **jib** tightly, and the helmsman must steer according to the **telltales**. **Bear away** if the **windward** telltales lift; **luff** slightly if the **leeward** ones lift.

TILLER •
Try to keep **tiller** movements gentle.

• MAINSAIL
If it is not too windy, **sheet in**. If you are overpowered by sudden gusts, either try **pinching** a little, or easing the sheet.

CHECKLIST OF ESSENTIALS

Whenever you alter sail **trim**, boat balance, **fore** and **aft** trim, **centerboard** position, or course, check the remaining 4 points and make any necessary adjustments to them.
• SAIL TRIM Ease the sail out and **sheet in** until it stops flapping.
• BOAT BALANCE Keep the boat flat.

• FORE AND AFT TRIM Adjust body weight distribution to avoid making waves.
• CENTERBOARD POSITION Raise or lower the **centerboard** to achieve a compromise between **drive** and **drag**.
• COURSE MADE GOOD Finally, keep an eye on your goal, and your route to it.

SKILL

DAY 2

11 CAPSIZING

Definition: *How to recover a boat when it has capsized*

All sailboats rely on helmsman and crew weight for stability so all sailboats are likely to capsize. The boat may be partially, or totally, inverted (pp.74–75), but recovery techniques are quite straightforward.

OBJECTIVE: To learn how to right a boat from the partially, and fully, inverted positions. *Rating* •••

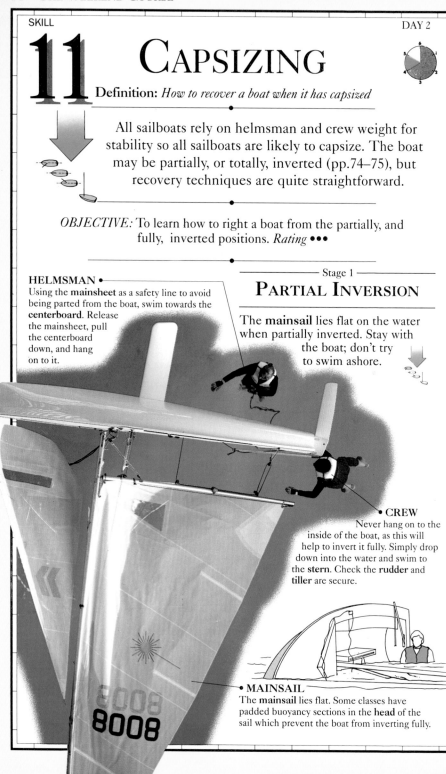

HELMSMAN •
Using the **mainsheet** as a safety line to avoid being parted from the boat, swim towards the **centerboard**. Release the mainsheet, pull the centerboard down, and hang on to it.

─── Stage 1 ───
PARTIAL INVERSION

The **mainsail** lies flat on the water when partially inverted. Stay with the boat; don't try to swim ashore.

• CREW
Never hang on to the inside of the boat, as this will help to invert it fully. Simply drop down into the water and swim to the **stern**. Check the **rudder** and **tiller** are secure.

• MAINSAIL
The **mainsail** lies flat. Some classes have padded buoyancy sections in the **head** of the sail which prevent the boat from inverting fully.

Stage 2

GETTING INTO POSTION

The aim is to scoop the crew aboard so he can assist and ensure that once righted, the boat cannot sail off leaving both people in the water.

SPEED OF RECOVERY
Recovery is slow at first, but once the **mainsail** is lifted clear of the water, the boat comes up much more quickly.

HELMSMAN •
When you reach the **centerboard**, wait for the crew to throw the **windward (top) jib sheet** over the hull. Grasp the jib sheet, then start to right the boat by leaning back flat in the water, with your feet against the lower **gunwale**. Keep your legs and back straight for maximum leverage and pull on the jib sheet.

CREW •
When the helmsman reaches the **centerboard**, swim along the inside of the boat to find the **windward (top) jib sheet**. Untangle it, and throw it over the top of the hull to the helmsman. Lie in the water alongside the boat, with your feet pointing towards the **stern**, and hold on to the hull or the toestraps. Do not put any weight on to the hull, or you might encourage the boat to invert fully.

8008

SKILL

11

THE SCOOP

HELMSMAN •
Standing on the root of the **centerboard**, where it comes out of the hull, lean back and pull steadily on the **jib sheet**. Have your back and legs straight for maximum leverage.

If the helmsman cannot right the boat by leaning back, she has to climb on to the **centerboard** and pull back from there.

ORIENTATION
When the boat has been capsized for long, the **rig** will drift to **windward** of the hull. The helmsman must pause as soon as the rig breaks clear of the water until the rig is blown **downwind** of the hull, or the boat will capsize again.

CREW •
At this stage, the crew's job is easy; lie and wait to be scooped into the boat as it is righted. While waiting, check that the paddle and bailing bucket haven't floated away and ensure that the **mainsheet** is slack, so that the **mainsail** can flap freely when the boat is uprighted.

TAKING THE WEIGHT
Not all **centerboards** are strong enough to withstand the full weight of the helmsman on their very tip. So it is always best to stand at the root of the board where it comes out of the hull. Ignore this and you could finish up with a bent, cracked or even a broken board.

TRAPPED

If you should be unlucky enough to find yourself underneath the **mainsail** or **jib** when the boat capsizes, do not panic. Push your hand up in the air to lift the sail and give yourself enough space to breathe. Then just swim out in any direction, still keeping your hand up. Before long, you will be clear of the sails, and you can start righting the boat, following all the techniques outlined in this skill.

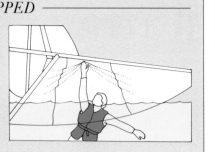

Stage 4

HELMSMAN ABOARD

The helmsman must now climb aboard at the **windward shroud**. If she attempts to board from the other side, the boat will capsize again. If she tries on the **windward** side, further **aft**, the boat will pivot and move off.

• JIB
As the helmsman used the **windward** (top) **jib sheet** to pull the boat upright, the boat is hove-to (see p.50), although the **tiller** might need a nudge from the crew to get it down to **leeward**.

• CREW
Balance the boat carefully when upright – if full of water, it might be unstable. Help the helmsman aboard at the **windward shroud**, and bail out.

MAINSAIL •
With the crew at the **windward shroud**, the **mainsail** will be flapping out of his way, balancing his weight while he helps the helmsman.

HELMSMAN •
Climb aboard at the **windward shroud**, tidy up, and then sail off again.

INSIDE THE BOAT •
Sort out all spare ropes and tidy the inside of the boat, before sailing on.

SKILL

11 TOTAL INVERSION

There is a growing tendency for boats to invert completely when they capsize. This is due to the way buoyancy is distributed in the sides of the hull rather than in the **bow** and **stern**. Once inverted, the boat is inherently stable and the resistance of the sails moving through water makes it slow to right. Recovery from total inversion is similar to that for partial inversion, but first you have to break the stability of the inverted boat and then bring it up to the better, partially-inverted position (see p.70) so that it can be fully righted.

Stage 1
BREAKING THE SEAL

HELMSMAN •
Find a **jib sheet** (preferably the **downwind** one) from underneath the hull. Climb on to the inverted hull holding the sheet. If it is not too windy, stand on the **windward gunwale** with your back to the wind, or kneel on the hull and pull backwards.

Some boat classes are best righted by putting weight at the stern (see below); others, by sinking the bow. Find out which technique is best for your class of boat before sailing.

• CREW
Crouch on the **stern**. Your combined weight starts the boat moving. Swim to the **centerboard** and help aboard the helmsman.

CENTERBOARD •
If possible, pull the **centerboard** into the fully lowered position. Otherwise you will have to right the boat by kneeling on the **gunwale**.

HELMSMAN •
As the boat slowly comes upright, you should be able to scramble from the **gunwale** to the **centerboard**, for a more secure position. If the **rig** comes up facing into the wind, pause when the **mast** is just clear of the water so that the whole boat swings until the rig is downwind.

Stage 2

RIGHTING THE BOAT

Due to water resistance on the **rig**, the boat takes a long time to right from the fully inverted to the partially inverted 90°position.

• **CREW**
During righting, beware of becoming separated from the boat: it will start to drift quickly in strong winds as it comes upright.

• **SAILS**
Tiredness may force you to lower the **mainsail** before righting the boat.

MAST STUCK
If the **mast** gets stuck on the bottom in shallow water you'll need to call for help .

12 MAN OVERBOARD

Definition: *When one member of the crew falls from the boat into the water*

KNOWING HOW TO RECOVER AN MOB (man overboard) is useful when sailing, for obvious reasons. But it is more than that. Mastery of this skill shows that you understand all the principles involved in controlling the speed and direction of your boat.

OBJECTIVE: To return under control to a spot in the water, stop, and recover a man overboard. *Rating* ● ● ● ●

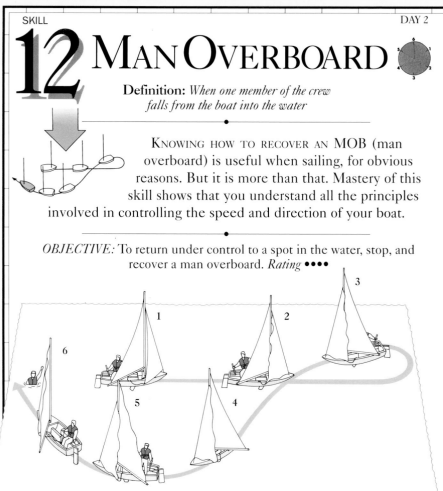

THE RECOVERY SEQUENCE

The basic technique used to recover an MOB consists of 6 steps. The sequence is always the same, regardless of the course you are on when the person falls into the water.

1. Start by regaining control of the boat, and getting on to a **beam reach**. Signal or call to the MOB that you will be back in a few minutes. Let the **jib** flap, and ensure that the **centerboard** is about half to three-quarters down.

2. Sail away far enough so that you can make your approach in the right direction under control – between 10 and 15 boat-lengths. Give yourself plenty of room to get down to **leeward** ready for the next stage.

3. **Tack** round on to the reciprocal beam reach. Make sure that you have the MOB still in sight before proceeding.

4. Bear away on to a **broad reach** far enough to make your approach on a **close reach**.

5. Close reaching is the only point of sailing that allows perfect control over your speed and direction. If you are coming in too quickly or too slowly, use the **mainsheet** to control power.

6. Make your final approach, intending to stop the boat when the MOB is at the **windward shroud**, where you can help him back aboard. If you try to pick him up on the **leeward** side of the boat, you will probably end up with the boat capsized and both of you in the water. If you try to pick him up further **aft** than the shroud, the boat may pivot around the MOB and start sailing away again. Get the position right and the boat will sit quietly, with the sails flapping out of the way, while you retrieve him.

MASTERING THE TECHNIQUE

RECOGNIZE A BEAM REACH

If you end too far to **windward** during the return to the MOB, it will be impossible to stop, so you must learn to recognize when you are on the correct **beam reach**: the waves should be at right angles to the boat, and your wind indicator – if you have one – streaming across the boat.

PRACTICE THE MANEUVER

Sail into any quiet area of water that is clear of moorings and other boats, and practice with a dummy. A large (at least 25 liter/6 gallon) plastic container almost filled with water makes an excellent substitute MOB, which will drift in a similar way to a real one.

HELMSMAN •
Move to the **windward shroud**. If you cannot get the MOB into the boat unaided, use a loop of rope as a footstep.

Stage 6

RETRIEVING THE MOB

Heave the MOB aboard at the **windward shroud**.

TILLER •
Give the **tiller** extension a quick flick to **windward**, just before you leave it to retrieve the MOB. Doing this ensures that the boat does not **luff**, an action that might lead to it **tacking** on top of the MOB.

SAILS •
The sails flap idly out of the way of the helmsman, making it unlikely that the boat will be able to sail anywhere of its own accord.

AFTER THE WEEKEND

Now you have mastered the basics, you can be more adventurous

WELL DONE! In just two days you have learned the principal techniques of sailing. Whether you stay with boats or progress to sailing yachts, all you have covered in the weekend will be relevant. So what is next?

Joining a Club

Belonging to a sailing club has many advantages. You can use the club's boats, and practice your sailing skills by crewing for someone who owns a boat. If you decide that you want to buy your own boat, the club may be able to help you to choose and find a boat second-hand.

Before joining a club, and especially if there are several near your home, find out what facilities and activities are offered so that you can choose the club that suits you best. In some clubs, members are asked to perform certain duties both afloat and ashore; for example taking turns to man the rescue boat, or helping in the clubhouse.

Competitive Sailing

Racing is the main activity in many sailing clubs. It is a good way of learning to cope with other craft, and of familiarizing yourself with the basic rules of the sea. Although the top competitors have regular helmsman/crew partnerships, on most club sailing days there is usually someone looking for a crew.

Special Courses

An alternative way to learn about racing is to go on a race training course at a club, sailing school or sailing center, which will teach you the rules and tactics, plus more advanced sailing techniques like roll **tacking**, roll **jibing**, and sailing in strong winds (see pp.80-85).

Solitary Sailing

Even if you do not like clubs, you can still enjoy sailing. Some people get enough excitement from a two-week holiday to last the whole year. Others prefer the quieter, more relaxed pastime of solitary cruising. That, after all, is the beauty of the sport: it is what you make it.

ROLL TACKING

A light weather technique to speed up your tacks

LEARN THIS MANEUVER as soon as you have mastered **tacking**. The basic technique covers both center- and **aft-mainsheet** sailboats: the only difference is the direction in which the helmsman faces during the **tack**.

4

3

2

1

THE MANEUVER

To turn from sailing **close-hauled** in one direction to the other, start the **tack** (1) as before (see pp. 42–7), but when the boat is **head-to-wind** (2), lean out hard in the direction of the turn. Cross to the new **windward** side (3) only when the boat is almost on its new, close-hauled course (4).

——— Stage 2 ———

HEAD TO WIND

Having borne away to ensure maximum speed, the helmsman initiated the **tack** by calling "Ready About" and pushing the **tiller** firmly away. The roll starts now.

HELMSMAN AND CREW •
When the boat is **head-to-wind**, the crew moves to the old **windward** side and, with the helmsman, leans out hard. This makes the boat **heel** right over. You have mastered the technique when the **gunwale** reaches the water.

TILLER •
Keep the **tiller** held over firmly throughout the whole maneuver.

• SAILS
By rolling the hull, you increase the apparent wind passing over the sails, and therefore speed up the boat.

Stage 4

SETTING THE COURSE

HELMSMAN AND CREW •
As the boat nears a **close-hauled** course on the new **tack**, cross simultaneously to the **windward** side to bring the boat upright again. In very light winds, only the helmsman will cross; the crew remains seated on the new **leeward** side.

A common mistake at this stage is to cross to the new side too soon. Wait until the boat is at least halfway between the **head-to-wind** and **close-hauled** positions before making your move.

SAILS •
Initially, ease both sails in the light wind, then **sheet** them in smoothly again as the boat accelerates.

TILLER •
Straighten the **tiller** as the boat assumes the new course, but do not change hands until you have completed the maneuver.

WINDSHIFTS

WORK WITH WIND
Athough the wind may appear to be coming from a single direction, it often veers slightly, especially when it is light.
• Windshifts have the most effect when you are sailing **upwind**. If sailing **close-hauled** on a course (blue arrow) for the buoy, the problem arises if the wind shifts so that it is blowing from further ahead (black arrow). The sails then start to lift and the boat becomes more upright.
• If the shift is more than temporary, you can reach the buoy only by **bearing away** until the sails start to fill again, and then putting in a couple of extra **tacks**.
• Look out for favorable windshifts, which allow you either to ease the sails, or point higher, thus making it easier for you to reach your target.

ROLL JIBING

In light weather, improve your jibe with a roll

IF YOU JIBE IN LIGHT WINDS following the usual technique (see pp.60–65), it takes a long time for the boat to turn through a wide enough arc for the **mainsail** to fill from the other side and be blown across the boat. Roll jibing speeds up the process. The technique can be used in both center-**mainsheet** and aft-mainsheet sailboats.

JIBING SEQUENCE

The approach (**1**) is the same as with a normal **jibe**, but when the jibe is initiated (**2**), the crew moves over quickly but smoothly to the helms-man's side. This rolls the boat (**3**), bringing the **boom** over to the new **leeward** side. The helmsman then changes sides and sails off on the new course (**4**).

1

2

3

4

──── Stage 2 ────

STARTING TO JIBE

Have the boat flat to begin with: it is hard to **bear away** with the boat **heeled** to **leeward**. The helmsman checks that the area into which you will sail is clear, and warns the crew by saying "Ready to jibe?".

HELMSMAN AND CREW •
As the helmsman pulls the **tiller** to **windward** to initiate the turn, and calls "Jibe-ho", the crew moves to the windward side and, in one fluid movement, they both lean out to pull the boat over on top of them.

MAINSAIL •
By pulling across the **kicking strap**, the crew causes the **boom**, and hence the sails, to swing over to the other side of the boat.

• TILLER
Straighten the **tiller** in mid-**jibe**, when the **stern** of the boat passes through the wind, and the **boom** swings across.

Stage 4
NEW COURSE SETTING

• HELMSMAN
Having crossed to the new **windward** side, continue to steer with the old hand until the boat is properly settled down on the new course. Then change hands on the **mainsheet** and **tiller**.

As the **boom** swings across during the **jibe**, the helmsman starts to move across on to the new **windward** side to bring the boat upright again. After that, the technique is exactly the same as you learned earlier for jibing. Once on your new course, **trim** the sails and adjust the **centerboard**.

• CENTERBOARD
Following on from the **jibe**, adjust the **centerboard** to the new course you are sailing.

CREW •
Continue sitting to **leeward** to balance the boat, unless the new course is far enough **upwind** to require your weight to **windward**.

• SAILS
Trim the sails for the new course, first setting the **jib** according to the **telltales** and then trimming the **mainsail** until it just stops flapping along the **luff**.

CHOOSING A COURSE IN LIGHT WINDS

POINTS TO CONSIDER
Choosing the most efficient course between two points can be tricky, especially in light winds.
• When sailing **offwind** in non-tidal waters, you will reach your goal simply by setting a course and heading straight towards your destination.
• In a tide or current, however, make allowances for the stream setting you either **upwind** or **downwind** of your goal.
• When sailing upwind, take account of wind shifts. Watch out for obstructions.

TIDES AND CURRENTS
• Try to stay in the best of a favorable stream, where the flow of the tide will assist your progress.
• Conversely, try to stay out of the worst of a foul stream, where the tide will be running against you.
• Remember that tides and currents flow fastest in the middle of rivers and channels.
• However, mid-channel may be where you have the safest depth of water to prevent you going aground.

SAILING IN STRONG WINDS

Mastering this technique will enable you to handle heavy weather when sailing both upwind and downwind

As YOU GAIN MORE CONFIDENCE, you will want to venture out in stronger winds and experience the sheer thrill of sailing a powerful, lightweight boat in such conditions. Everything happens faster, and you will find that the boat is less forgiving of your errors.

UPWIND

Sailing **upwind** in strong winds is physically demanding, as you need to balance the much stronger **heeling** effect of the wind on the **rig**.

• CREW
Sit out hard to keep the boat flat, and move slightly **aft** from your normal **upwind** position to help the **bow** lift.

• SAILS
Flatten the **mainsail** by pulling harder on the **downhaul** and **outhaul**. In the gusts, ease both sails very gently until there is just a hint of flapping at the **luff**.

• CENTERBOARD
Raise the **centerboard** a little, even when beating, to reduce the **heeling** forces. Your extra speed compensates for any additional **leeway**.

HELMSMAN •
Steer the boat through each wave. Point high as you climb and pull in the **mainsheet**, then ease the mainsheet slightly and **bear away** down into the next trough. As you go down the waves, be ready to move **aft** to stop the **bow** burying into the water.

HELMSMAN •
Sit well aft as you surf or **plane** down the waves but avoid digging in the **stern**. Keep the **mainsail** full, coordinate **tiller** and **sheet** movements, and never try to **bear away** without easing the **sheet**, or you may break the **rudder**.

DOWNWIND

The boat shown here is on a **broad reach**, but all points (except crew position) apply equally to **running**.

• **CREW**
The boat will **plane** only if it is flat, so sit close to the helmsman to **trim** the boat **fore** and **aft**. On a **run**, sit to **leeward**. Trim the boat to keep the **bow** clear of the next wave.

SAILS •
If the wind overpowers you, ease the **kicking strap** to free off the **leech** and spill wind from the upper part of the **mainsail**. Move adjustable **jib fairleads** aft and outboard to open the slot between jib and mainsail. Never oversheet the jib: it will stall and lose power.

• **CENTERBOARD**
Raise the **centerboard** until it is only one third down to stop the boat tripping over it at the end of each surfing or **planing** ride.

• **TILLER**
Luff up in the lulls and **bear away** in the gusts. Bear away as each wave lifts your **stern**, then luff as you go down the wave to prolong the ride.

THE EXCITEMENT OF PLANING

RIDING THE WAVES
Planing is when the boat lifts up on its **bow** wave. The lighter and more powerful the boat, the more readily it will plane.
• The boat must first be sailing flat. Have the **centerboard** half-raised. It is easiest to start when you are on a **reach**.
• To initiate planing, watch for a gust, sit out hard, and be ready to ease the **sheets** to balance the increase in **heeling** force.

• When the gust hits the boat and the bow starts to lift, move your weight **aft** and concentrate on keeping the boat flat. As the boat accelerates, **sheet in** to keep the sails full, lean out, and enjoy the ride.
• When the gust starts to die away, you can prolong planing by **luffing** slightly. As the boat comes off the plane, however, move your weight forward. Watch the wind and the waves and be ready for the next gust.

BASIC RULES OF THE SEA

Know how to react when you meet other craft afloat

ALL CRAFT FOLLOW the International Regulations for Preventing Collisions at Sea (IRPCS), which govern right of way. When you meet other sailing craft, the two fundamental rules outlined opposite apply. If the other vessel is a power craft of similar size, you have right of way, and should maintain your course and speed.

RACING TACTICS

Your aim, when racing, is to get around the course in the shortest time, by steering the fastest route between the buoys marking each leg of the course. When 2 boats are close together (like these Lasers below), the "same tack" rule prevents the **windward** boat coming too close to the **leeward** one, and gives the latter a chance to protect her clear wind.

RULES FOR COMPETITIVE SAILING

Most congestion occurs at the rounding marks. When these 2 boats come together at the next mark with all the others in their race, a complex series of rules, laid down by the International Yacht Racing Union, governs their behavior in close quarters.

FUNDAMENTAL RULE 1:
FOR BOATS ON OPPOSITE TACKS

The boat with the wind on her **port** side must give way to the one with the wind on her **starboard** side. The boat on starboard **tack** is obliged to maintain her course and speed. The boat on port tack has 3 options: to slow down and wait for the other to pass ahead; to **bear away**, thus passing **astern**; or to tack.

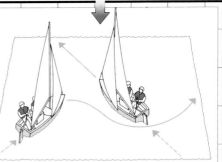

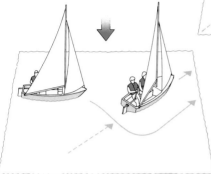

FUNDAMENTAL RULE 2:
FOR BOATS ON THE SAME TACK

The boat to **windward** must give way to the one to **leeward**. The reason for this rule is obvious: if the windward boat gets too close, it will take all the wind – and hence the power – from the leeward craft, which will then be unable to maneuver. When one boat is overtaking another, the overtaking craft must keep clear of the other boat.

ENCOUNTERING LARGE VESSELS

The old adage that steam should give way to sail applies only when a power-driven and a sailing boat of roughly the same size meet each other. It is certainly not true in locations where a sailboat is likely to encounter a ship. The IRPCS state clearly that a ship maneuvering in a narrow channel should not be impeded by other craft. Common sense alone will tell you to give larger, more powerful vessels a wide berth.

MARKING YOUR BOOM

When a sailboat approaches you unexpectedly, it is easy to forget on which **tack** you are sailing. Jog your memory by marking your **boom** "port give way, starboard OK", as shown below.

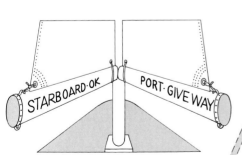

If the **boom** is on the **starboard** side, you are on **port tack**, and must give way to other sailing craft. If the boom is to port, you are on starboard tack, and have right of way.

CHOOSING A SAILBOAT

How to decide which class of sailboat is suitable for you

HUNDREDS OF SAILBOAT CLASSES are sailed around the world. Some conform to International Rules and are raced up to National and World Championship level; others are purely local classes. Before you buy, two questions will help to narrow your choice: "Where am I going to sail?" and "What form will my sailing take?" The classes shown on the opposite page are some of the most popular.

ROUND-BILGE HULL

Most of the classes designed for GRP construction in the past 20 years are round-bilge, and have buoyancy built in. The flatter the boat, the more likely it is to have been designed for racing. Rigs range from simple to very complex. Their super-efficient controls are geared to adjusting sail shape and power in different weather conditions. To learn the basic techniques, start in one of the classes that does not have these complications.

HARD-CHINE HULL

Many classes designed originally for wooden construction have hard-chine hulls. Most are now available also in GRP or in composite form (a GRP hull and wooden deck). The deeper the boat, the more likely it is to have been conceived as a general purpose or cruising boat, yet these classes may also be raced. Two people can sail a boat that is 4m (13ft) long. For 3 or 4 people, look for a 5m (16ft) boat.

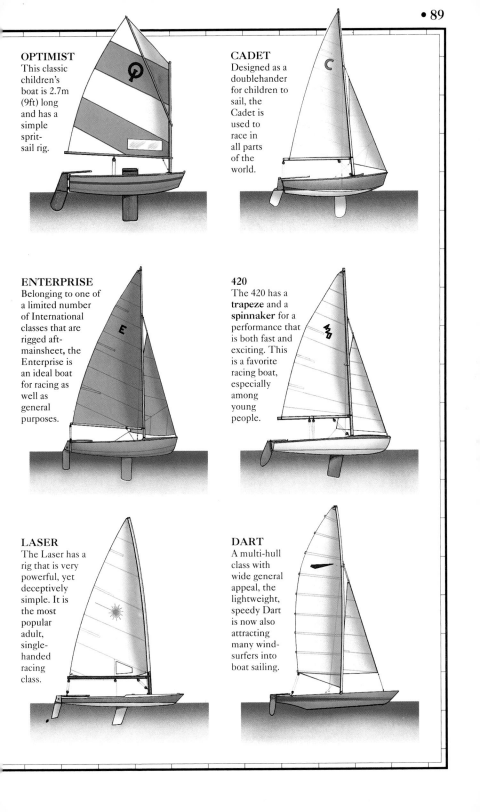

OPTIMIST
This classic children's boat is 2.7m (9ft) long and has a simple sprit-sail rig.

CADET
Designed as a doublehander for children to sail, the Cadet is used to race in all parts of the world.

ENTERPRISE
Belonging to one of a limited number of International classes that are rigged aft-mainsheet, the Enterprise is an ideal boat for racing as well as general purposes.

420
The 420 has a **trapeze** and a **spinnaker** for a performance that is both fast and exciting. This is a favorite racing boat, especially among young people.

LASER
The Laser has a rig that is very powerful, yet deceptively simple. It is the most popular adult, single-handed racing class.

DART
A multi-hull class with wide general appeal, the lightweight, speedy Dart is now also attracting many wind-surfers into boat sailing.

BUYING SECOND-HAND

Points and pitfalls to consider when buying a second-hand boat

SAILING MAGAZINES and club notice-boards are the best places to look for second-hand boat advertisements. If you know which class of boat you want, contact the class owners' association. They will tell you which clubs sail that class as fleets, and let you have a copy of the latest class magazine, which lists second-hand boats for sale. Before you buy, inspect the craft carefully, bearing in mind the main points detailed here. Minor defects, such as cracks in the hull, can be repaired, and worn **rigging** can be replaced. The price should reflect any imperfections.

JIB •
Wear is most apparent along the **leech** and at the corners. The strengthening panels around the **clew** should be firmly stitched. Feel the **luff** wire for kinks, which can weaken the sail.

MAINSAIL •
Look for wear at the corners, especially the **head**, and at the **batten** pockets, and check that the stitching is not coming undone. Make sure that the sail number, indicating the age of the boat, matches the number on the hull and the measurement certificate.

DECK •
A well cared-for boat will have been kept under a specially made cover. Inspect wooden decks for discoloration, which may lead to rot. GRP decks must have no fine cracks.

RIGGING •
Inspect for wear and rusting. Run your fingers along **shrouds** and metal **halyards** to feel for broken strands: these are often the first signs of trouble. Check rope halyards and other lines for fraying. Make sure that all fittings are secure.

CENTERBOARD •
Lower the **centerboard** to inspect for cracks. A damaged leading edge suggests that the boat had been run aground harshly. Ensure that the board is a tight fit within its case and that it does not wobble on the hinge bolt.

BUOYANCY
If buoyancy is built in, ask to see the result of the latest buoyancy test. Buoyancy bags should be hard, and the webbing straps that hold them in place unworn: you must be able to lift the boat by any one of them. If buoyancy tanks are fitted, check for leaks.

DOLLY AND TRAILER •
A galvanized dolly will last longer than a painted one. Look for signs of corrosion. Check trailer tires for uneven wear: checking each side of the trailer in turn, grasp the wheel and rock from side to side to check for worn bearings.

HULL •
Lift the boat off its dolly on to grass or another smooth surface. Turn it on to its side and make a close inspection for cracks and repair patches. Check the bottom of the hull, and then the other side. If the cracks are superficial, it is easy to rub down or fill them.

RUDDER AND TILLER •
Look for cracks in the **rudder** blade and stock and damage to the leading edge. Any looseness in the rudder hangings that is not due to loose bolts will cause trouble. Ensure that the **tiller** is a tight fit in the rudder and that the tiller extension moves freely.

GLOSSARY

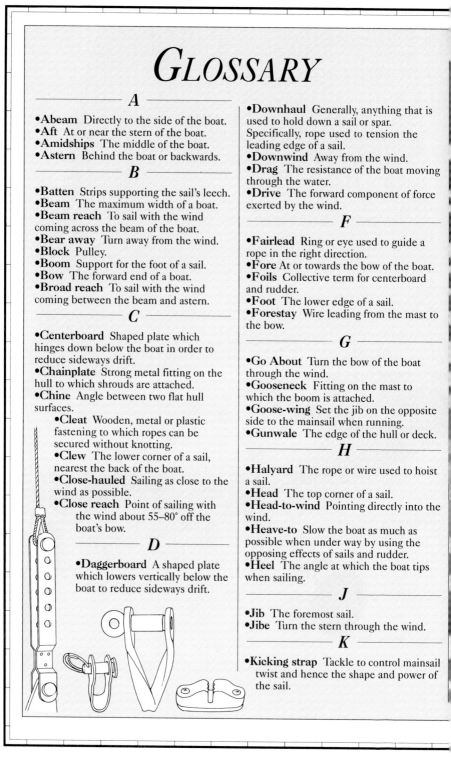

A

•**Abeam** Directly to the side of the boat.
•**Aft** At or near the stern of the boat.
•**Amidships** The middle of the boat.
•**Astern** Behind the boat or backwards.

B

•**Batten** Strips supporting the sail's leech.
•**Beam** The maximum width of a boat.
•**Beam reach** To sail with the wind coming across the beam of the boat.
•**Bear away** Turn away from the wind.
•**Block** Pulley.
•**Boom** Support for the foot of a sail.
•**Bow** The forward end of a boat.
•**Broad reach** To sail with the wind coming between the beam and astern.

C

•**Centerboard** Shaped plate which hinges down below the boat in order to reduce sideways drift.
•**Chainplate** Strong metal fitting on the hull to which shrouds are attached.
•**Chine** Angle between two flat hull surfaces.
  •**Cleat** Wooden, metal or plastic fastening to which ropes can be secured without knotting.
  •**Clew** The lower corner of a sail, nearest the back of the boat.
  •**Close-hauled** Sailing as close to the wind as possible.
  •**Close reach** Point of sailing with the wind about 55–80° off the boat's bow.

D

•**Daggerboard** A shaped plate which lowers vertically below the boat to reduce sideways drift.

•**Downhaul** Generally, anything that is used to hold down a sail or spar. Specifically, rope used to tension the leading edge of a sail.
•**Downwind** Away from the wind.
•**Drag** The resistance of the boat moving through the water.
•**Drive** The forward component of force exerted by the wind.

F

•**Fairlead** Ring or eye used to guide a rope in the right direction.
•**Fore** At or towards the bow of the boat.
•**Foils** Collective term for centerboard and rudder.
•**Foot** The lower edge of a sail.
•**Forestay** Wire leading from the mast to the bow.

G

•**Go About** Turn the bow of the boat through the wind.
•**Gooseneck** Fitting on the mast to which the boom is attached.
•**Goose-wing** Set the jib on the opposite side to the mainsail when running.
•**Gunwale** The edge of the hull or deck.

H

•**Halyard** The rope or wire used to hoist a sail.
•**Head** The top corner of a sail.
•**Head-to-wind** Pointing directly into the wind.
•**Heave-to** Slow the boat as much as possible when under way by using the opposing effects of sails and rudder.
•**Heel** The angle at which the boat tips when sailing.

J

•**Jib** The foremost sail.
•**Jibe** Turn the stern through the wind.

K

•**Kicking strap** Tackle to control mainsail twist and hence the shape and power of the sail.

L

•**Leech** The aft edge of a sail.
•**Leeward** The side away from the wind.
•**Leeway** Difference between course steered and course made good.
•**Luff** Forward edge of a sail. **Luff up** To turn towards the wind.

M

•**Mainsail** The large sail set on the mast.
•**Mainsheet** Rope for trimming mainsail
•**Mast** Vertical spar supporting the sails.

N

•**No-go area** Area into which a boat cannot sail directly. Goal can only be reached by tacking.

O

•**Offshore wind** One which blows from the land towards the water.
•**Offwind** Any direction away from wind.
•**Onshore wind** One which blows from the water on to the land.
•**Outhaul** Rope tackle used to tension the **foot** of the sail.

P

•**Painter** Rope attached to bow, by which the boat may be secured.
•**Pinching** Sailing too close to the wind.
•**Plane** Sail quickly in strong winds by pushing up over the bow wave.
•**Pointing ability** Upwind sailing efficiency. A boat is said to point high when it can sail very close to the wind.
•**Port** The left hand side of a boat when looking towards the bow.
•**Port tack** When the wind is coming over the port side of the boat, or when the **mainsail** is set to starboard.

R

•**Reach** To sail across the wind.
•**Reef** To reduce the size of the sails in strong winds.
•**Rigging** Collective term for wires and ropes which support the **spars** (standing **rigging**) and allow the sails to be controlled (running **rigging**).
•**Rudder** Blade at the stern which is angled to steer the boat.
•**Run** Sail directly away from the wind.

S

•**Sheet** Rope used to trim a sail. **Sheet in.** To pull in the sheet, adjusting the position of the sails.
•**Shrouds** Lateral wire supports for mast.
•**Spars** Collective term used for the masts and booms.
•**Spinnaker** Large lightweight triangular sail set when sailing offwind.
•**Starboard** The right hand side of the boat when looking towards the bow.
•**Starboard tack** When the wind is coming over the starboard side of the boat or when the mainsail is set to port.
•**Stern** The back of the boat.

T

•**Tack** The lower forward corner of a sail or turn the bow through the wind.
•**Telltales** Strips of ribbon used to check airflow over the sails accurately.
•**Tiller** Lever attached to rudder by which the boat is steered.
•**Transom** Flat surface at the back of the hull, to which the rudder is attached.
•**Trapeze** System allowing more leverage by getting further outboard.
•**Trim** The fore-and-aft angle of the boat in the water. Also term used for adjusting the sails as the wind changes.

U

•**Upwind** Towards the wind.

W

•**Warp** A rope used to secure a boat.
•**Windward** The side towards the wind.

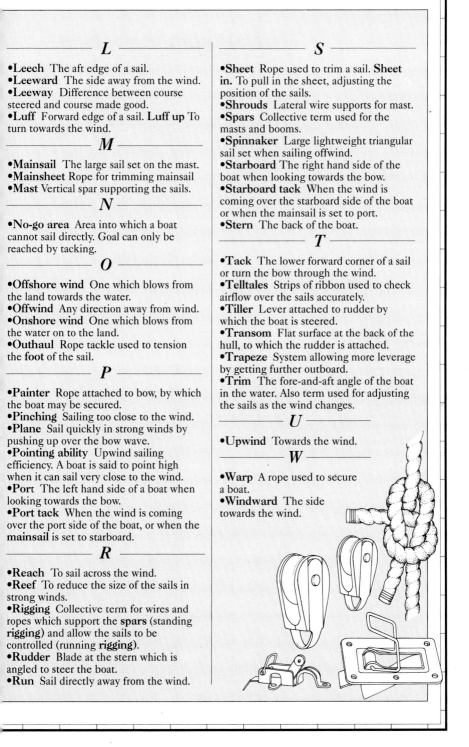

INDEX

ACKNOWLEDGMENTS

John Driscoll and Dorling Kindersley would like to thank the following for their help and support in the preparation and production of this book.

Adrian Jones of the Laser Centre, Banbury, Oxfordshire for the loan of a Laser 2 sailboat for the majority of the photo sequences. Joy Routledge and Paul Dobner for their patience in crewing the Laser 2. Colin Merrett of Racing Sailboats, London SW11 for the loan of clothes. Mike Gasken and Reg Carter of Thames Young Mariners, Richmond, Surrey for their assistance in boat storage. Chadwick Beecher-Moore and the staff of Jack Holt Ltd, Putney, London SW15 for the loan of an International Enterprise. The Flag Officers and Secretariat of Queen Mary Sailing Club, Ashford, Middlesex, for their cooperation in providing facilities. The Sports Council and staff of the National Sports Centre, Crystal Palace, London SE19 for their assistance. Roger Lean-Vercoe for the photograph on page 8. Jim Stoddart, Pip Tyler and the staff of Falcon Sailing, Bitez, Turkey for the photo of the author. Peter Blum of Meyer International for his assistance with location site. Tony Randall, Paul Bailey and Janos Marffy, for the illustrations; Tracy Hambilton for design assistance; Gillian Prince for editorial assistance.